FAMILY FAVORITES

Culinary Arts Institute.
A DIVISION OF DELAIR PUBLISHING COMPANY INC.

Contents

Appetizers 5
Salads 9
Soups 14
Breads 22
Pasta & Grains 29
Vegetables 35
Meat 44
Poultry 56
Seafood 64
Desserts 72
Index 79

APPETIZERS

Sausage and Applesauce Appetizers

1 package (12 ounces) smoked link
   sausage, cut in 1-inch pieces
1 jar (15 ounces) applesauce
1 tablespoon caraway seed
1½ teaspoons instant minced onion

1. Broil sausage pieces until evenly browned.
2. Combine with applesauce, caraway seed, and onion. Put into a 1-quart casserole.
3. Bake, covered, at 250°F 2 hours. Serve with wooden picks.

About 32 appetizers

Baked Carrot Spread

1 cup grated carrot
1 cup mayonnaise
1 cup (4 ounces) grated Romano
   cheese
½ teaspoon garlic salt
½ teaspoon lemon pepper seasoning

1. Combine all ingredients in a 1-quart casserole.
2. Bake, uncovered, at 350°F 25 minutes, or until heated through. Serve with **assorted crackers.**

3 cups

Baked Mushrooms

1½ pounds fresh mushroom caps*
1 cup butter or margarine, melted
2 teaspoons finely chopped onion
1 garlic clove, minced
½ teaspoon rosemary
¾ teaspoon Worcestershire sauce

1. Place mushroom caps in a 1½-quart casserole.
2. Combine remaining ingredients. Pour over mushrooms.
3. Bake, covered, at 325°F 30 minutes, or until tender.

12 servings

* The mushroom stems can be sautéed and added to **hot, cooked green beans.**

Onion Appetizers

4 medium onions, finely chopped
3 tablespoons butter or margarine
½ cup dairy sour cream
1 tablespoon flour
½ teaspoon salt
   Dash pepper
1 teaspoon caraway seed
3 eggs, beaten
4 bacon slices, cooked and crumbled
1 unbaked 9-inch pie shell

1. Sauté onion in butter in a skillet.
2. Blend sour cream, flour, salt, pepper, and caraway seed. Beat in eggs. Stir in bacon and onion. Pour into pie shell.
3. Bake, uncovered, at 325°F 35 to 40 minutes, or until filling is set. Let stand a few minutes. Cut into wedges to serve.

16 appetizers

Wine-Cheese Canapés

½ cup whipped unsalted butter
4 teaspoons Roquefort cheese
4 toasted bread rounds
2 packages (3 ounces each) cream
  cheese
2 tablespoons sauterne
  Parsley, minced
  Pimento-stuffed olive slices
  Paprika
  Clear Glaze (see recipe)

1. Whip together butter and Roquefort cheese. Spread onto toasted bread rounds.
2. Whip cream cheese with sauterne.
3. Pipe a swirl of the mixture onto each canapé. Roll edges in minced parsley. Top with pimento-stuffed olive slice; sprinkle with paprika.
4. Glaze and chill.

Clear Glaze: Soften **1 envelope unflavored gelatin** in ⅔ **cup cold water** in a bowl. Pour **1 cup boiling water** over softened gelatin and stir until gelatin is dissolved. Chill until slightly thickened. To glaze canapés: Place canapés on wire racks over a large shallow pan. Working quickly, spoon about 2 teaspoons of slightly thickened gelatin over each canapé. (Have ready a bowl of ice and water and a bowl of hot water. The gelatin may have to be set over one or the other during glazing to maintain the proper consistency.) The gelatin should cling slightly to canapés when spooned over them. Any drips may be scooped up and reused.

About 24 canapés

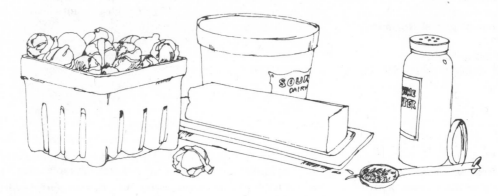

Liver Pâté

This is not baked, but made with gelatin and chilled. Calories can be cut by serving with vegetables rather than the usual crackers.

1½ cups chopped onion
1 cup chopped celery
1½ cups Chicken Stock
1 cup dry white wine
1 teaspoon paprika
⅛ teaspoon ground allspice or
  cloves
¼ teaspoon garlic powder
4 drops Tabasco
1¼ teaspoons salt
1½ pounds chicken livers,
  membranes removed
2 envelopes unflavored gelatin
½ cup cold water
  Assorted vegetable relishes

1. Simmer onion and celery in stock and wine in an uncovered saucepan until liquid is reduced to 2 cups (about 15 minutes). Stir in paprika, allspice, garlic powder, Tabasco, and salt; simmer 2 minutes. Stir in livers; simmer covered until livers are tender (about 15 minutes). Drain; discard liquid.
2. Sprinkle gelatin over cold water; let stand 3 minutes. Set over low heat, stirring occasionally, until gelatin is dissolved (about 5 minutes).
3. Purée half the livers and vegetables along with half the gelatin mixture in a food processor or blender. Repeat with remaining ingredients; combine the two mixtures.
4. Pour mixture into a lightly oiled 1½-quart mold or bowl or ten 6-ounce custard cups. Chill until set (about 4 hours).
5. Serve from mold, or unmold onto platter and accompany with assorted vegetables.

10 to 12 servings

Puff Shrimp with Orange Ginger Sauce

Orange Ginger Sauce (see recipe)
Fat for deep frying heated to 375°F

2 pounds medium raw shrimp (20 to 25 per pound)
3 egg yolks
½ cup white wine
¾ cup all-purpose flour
1 teaspoon salt
¼ teaspoon pepper
3 egg whites

Orange Ginger Sauce:
1 cup orange marmalade
2 tablespoons soy sauce
¼ cup sherry
1 piece whole ginger root
1 clove garlic, minced

1. Prepare and cool Orange Ginger Sauce.
2. Fill a deep saucepan or automatic deep fryer one-half to two-thirds full with fat for deep frying; heat slowly to 375°F.
3. Shell and devein raw shrimp and set aside.
4. Beat together in a bowl egg yolks, wine, flour, salt, and pepper until smooth.
5. Beat egg whites until stiff, not dry, peaks are formed. Fold egg whites into egg yolk mixture.
6. Dry shrimp thoroughly and dip into batter, coating well.
7. Deep-fry one layer deep in heated fat 2 to 3 minutes on each side, or until golden brown. Remove from fat with a slotted spoon. Drain on absorbent paper. Be sure temperature of fat is 375°F before frying each layer. Serve shrimp hot accompanied with the Orange Ginger Sauce for dipping.
8. For Orange Ginger Sauce, combine in a saucepan marmalade, soy sauce, sherry, ginger root, and minced garlic. Stir over low heat until mixture bubbles. Remove from heat. Cool. Remove ginger before serving.

40 to 50 appetizers

Oysters Rockefeller

2 tablespoons butter or margarine
2 tablespoons flour
½ teaspoon salt
⅛ teaspoon pepper
1 cup milk (use light cream for richer sauce)
1 egg, well beaten
2 dozen oysters in shells
2 tablespoons sherry
2 tablespoons butter or margarine
1 tablespoon finely chopped onion
1 pound fresh spinach, cooked, drained, and finely chopped
1 tablespoon minced parsley
½ teaspoon Worcestershire sauce
6 drops Tabasco
¼ teaspoon salt
Few grains ground nutmeg
¼ cup shredded Parmesan cheese

1. For sauce, heat 2 tablespoons butter in a saucepan. Blend in flour, salt, and pepper; heat and stir until bubbly.
2. Gradually add the milk, stirring until smooth. Bring to boiling; cook and stir 1 to 2 minutes longer.
3. Stir the egg into white sauce; set aside.
4. Pour **coarse salt** into a 15×10×1-inch jelly roll pan to a ¼-inch depth. Open oysters and arrange the oysters, in the shells, on the salt; sprinkle ¼ teaspoon sherry over each.
5. Heat 2 tablespoons butter in a heavy skillet. Add the onion and cook until partially tender. Add the chopped spinach, 2 tablespoons of the white sauce, parsley, Worcestershire sauce, and Tabasco to the skillet along with salt and nutmeg; mix thoroughly. Heat 2 to 3 minutes.
6. Spoon spinach mixture over all of the oysters; spoon remaining white sauce over spinach. Sprinkle each oyster with cheese.
7. Bake at 375°F 15 to 20 minutes, or until tops are lightly browned.

4 to 6 servings

Avocado Sandwiches on Sour Dough

2 avocados, thinly sliced and salted
¼ cup butter (½ stick), softened
½ teaspoon oregano leaves
¼ teaspoon each chervil, parsley flakes, and grated lemon peel
Dash onion powder
8 slices sour dough or Italian bread, diagonally cut

1. Prepare avocado slices.
2. Cream butter with seasonings. Spread thinly over bread.
3. Top with avocado slices. Serve with white wine.

8 servings

Wine-Pickled Mushrooms

1 **pound fresh mushrooms, sliced lengthwise**
1 **cup water**
⅔ **cup white vinegar**
½ **cup sugar**
1 **teaspoon salt**
½ **teaspoon monosodium gluta-mate**
½ **teaspoon celery salt**
4 **sprigs parsley**
2 **small stalks celery**
1 **tablespoon mixed pickling spices**
1 **bay leaf**
6 **whole cloves**
12 **peppercorns**
½ **teaspoon whole allspice**
1 **cup dry white wine**

1. Prepare mushrooms and set aside in a bowl.
2. Mix remaining ingredients, except wine, in a saucepan; bring rapidly to boiling, reduce heat and simmer 10 minutes.
3. Strain the mixture over mushrooms and stir in the wine.
4. Cover and refrigerate several days before serving.

1 quart pickled mushrooms

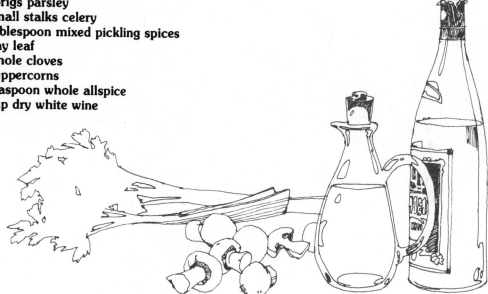

Cocktail Meatballs with Mushroom Curry Sauce

Meatballs:
1 **pound ground beef**
½ **cup fine soft bread crumbs**
¼ **cup milk**
¼ **cup sherry**
1 **egg, slightly beaten**
2 **tablespoons grated onion**
¼ **teaspoon ground ginger**
1 **teaspoon salt**
¼ **teaspoon pepper**
2 **tablespoons bacon drippings or other fat**

Mushroom Curry Sauce:
1 **can (about 10 ounces) condensed cream of mushroom soup**
¼ **cup sherry**
1 **teaspoon curry powder**

1. For meatballs, mix beef, bread crumbs, milk, wine, egg, onion, ginger, salt, and pepper; shape mixture into little balls, using about one level teaspoon for each.
2. Heat bacon drippings in a large heavy skillet; add a single layer of meatballs and cook, slowly, for about 10 minutes, or until meat is done, shaking pan gently from time to time to cook and brown evenly.
3. When all meat is cooked, spear each with a pick and arrange in hot serving dish.
4. For sauce, combine soup, wine, and curry powder. Heat through and serve piping hot with meatballs.

About 60 meatballs

SALADS

Bacon-Bean Salad

⅔ cup cider vinegar
¾ cup sugar
1 teaspoon salt
1 can (16 ounces) cut green beans
1 can (16 ounces) cut wax beans
1 can (16 ounces) kidney beans, thoroughly rinsed and drained
1 medium onion, quartered and finely sliced
1 medium green pepper, chopped
½ teaspoon freshly ground black pepper
⅓ cup salad oil
1 pound bacon, cut in 1-inch squares
Lettuce (optional)

1. Blend vinegar, sugar, and salt in a small saucepan. Heat until the sugar is dissolved and set aside.
2. Drain all beans and toss with onion, green pepper, vinegar mixture, and ground pepper. Pour oil over all and toss to coat evenly. Store in a covered container in refrigerator.
3. When ready to serve, fry bacon until crisp; drain on absorbent paper. Toss the bacon with bean mixture. If desired, serve the salad on crisp lettuce.

About 12 servings

Note: If desired, omit bacon.

Mixed Vegetable Salad

1 cup diced cooked potatoes
1½ cups cooked sliced carrots
1½ cups cooked whole or cut green beans (fresh, frozen, or canned)
1½ cups cooked green peas (fresh, frozen, or canned)
1 cup sliced or diced cooked beets
Bottled Italian-style salad dressing
Lettuce
1 cup sliced celery
1 small onion, chopped
2 hard-cooked eggs, chopped
¾ cup small pimento-stuffed olives
¾ cup mayonnaise
¼ cup chili sauce
1 teaspoon lemon juice

1. Put potatoes, carrots, beans, peas, and beets into separate bowls. Pour salad dressing over each vegetable; chill thoroughly.
2. To serve, drain vegetables and arrange in a lettuce-lined salad bowl along with celery, onion, eggs, and olives.
3. Blend mayonnaise, chili sauce, and lemon juice. Pass with the salad.

About 8 servings

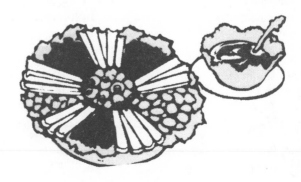

Tossed Supper Salad

Dressing:
- 1 cup salad oil
- ½ cup cider vinegar
- 1 teaspoon salt
- 1 teaspoon sugar
- ½ teaspoon onion salt
- ¼ teaspoon crushed tarragon
- ¼ teaspoon paprika
- ¼ teaspoon dry mustard
- ¼ teaspoon celery salt
- ⅛ teaspoon garlic salt
- ⅛ teaspoon ground black pepper

Salad:
- 2 cans (6½ or 7 ounces each) tuna
- ½ head lettuce
- 1 cup spinach leaves, washed
- 1 cup diced celery
- ¾ cup chopped green pepper
- ½ cup cooked green peas
- 4 sweet pickles, chopped
- 4 radishes, thinly sliced
- 2 hard-cooked eggs, sliced
- 2 tablespoons chopped pimento
- 2 tomatoes, rinsed and cut in eighths
- 1 teaspoon salt
- Tomato wedges
- Ripe olives

1. For dressing, put oil and vinegar into a jar; mix salt, sugar, and seasonings; add to jar, cover, and shake well. Refrigerate until needed. Shake before using.

2. For salad, drain tuna well and separate into small chunks; put into a bowl. Toss tuna with ½ cup prepared dressing; cover and refrigerate 1 to 2 hours.

3. Tear lettuce and spinach into pieces and put into a large bowl. Add celery, green pepper, peas, pickles, radishes, eggs, and pimento; add the tuna with its dressing and tomatoes. Sprinkle with salt. Toss lightly until ingredients are mixed and lightly coated with dressing; add more dressing, if desired.

4. Garnish with tomato wedges and ripe olives.

8 to 10 servings

Note: Two cups of diced cooked chicken, turkey, veal, or pork may be substituted for tuna.

Molded Spinach Cottage Cheese on Platter

- 1 package (10 ounces) frozen chopped spinach
- 2 envelopes unflavored gelatin
- ¾ cup water
- 2 chicken bouillon cubes
- 2 tablespoons lemon juice
- 1½ cups creamed cottage cheese
- ½ cup dairy sour cream
- ½ cup sliced celery
- ⅓ cup chopped green pepper
- 2 tablespoons minced green onion

1. Cook and drain spinach, reserving liquid. Add enough water to liquid to make ½ cup. Set spinach and liquid aside.

2. Soften gelatin in ¾ cup water in a saucepan; add bouillon cubes. Set over low heat; stirring occasionally, until gelatin and bouillon cubes are dissolved. Remove from heat; stir in spinach liquid and lemon juice. Set aside.

3. Beat cottage cheese until fairly smooth with mixer or in electric blender. Blend with sour cream and then gelatin mixture. Stir in spinach, celery, green pepper, and onion. Turn into a 5-cup mold. Chill until firm.

4. Unmold onto a chilled large platter. If desired, arrange slices of summer sausage around the mold.

6 to 8 servings

Garden-Green Salad Mold

1 package (3 ounces) lime-flavored
    gelatin
¼ teaspoon salt
1 cup boiling water
1 cup cold water
1 ripe medium avocado
1 tablespoon lemon juice
2 cups finely shredded cabbage
½ cup thinly sliced radishes
½ cup thinly sliced green onions with
    tops
    Crisp greens

1. Put gelatin and salt into a bowl; add boiling water and stir until completely dissolved. Blend in cold water. Chill until slightly thickened.
2. Mash avocado and stir in lemon juice; blend thoroughly with gelatin. Mix in cabbage, radishes, and green onions.
3. Turn into a 1-quart mold or individual molds and chill until firm. Unmold onto chilled serving plate and garnish with salad greens.

About 8 servings

Stewed Tomato Aspic

1 envelope unflavored gelatin
½ cup cold water
1 can (16 ounces) stewed tomatoes
1 tablespoon sugar
¼ teaspoon salt
1 tablespoon cider vinegar
1½ teaspoons prepared horseradish
1½ teaspoons grated onion
¼ teaspoon Worcestershire sauce
2 hard-cooked eggs, cut in quarters
    Salad greens

1. Sprinkle gelatin over water to soften.
2. Turn tomatoes into a saucepan and break up any large pieces with a spoon. Stir in sugar, salt, vinegar, horseradish, onion, and Worcestershire sauce and heat to boiling. Add softened gelatin and stir until dissolved.
3. Chill gelatin until slightly thickened.
4. Arrange egg quarters around bottom of a 3- or 4-cup mold. Spoon slightly thickened gelatin mixture into mold. Chill until firm.
5. Unmold and garnish with crisp greens.

4 to 6 servings

Rice Salad with Assorted Sausages

⅓ cup white wine vinegar
1 teaspoon lemon juice
¼ teaspoon French mustard
1 teaspoon salt
¼ teaspoon ground black pepper
⅓ cup salad oil
3 cups cooked enriched white rice,
    cooled
3 cups finely shredded red cabbage
½ cup raisins
½ cup walnut pieces
    Greens
    Link sausage (such as bratwurst,
    smoky links, and frankfurters),
    cooked

1. Put vinegar into a bottle. Add lemon juice, mustard, salt, and pepper. Cover and shake. Add oil and shake well.
2. Combine rice, cabbage, raisins, and walnuts in a bowl; chill.
3. When ready to serve, shake dressing well and pour over salad; toss until well mixed.
4. Arrange greens on luncheon plates, spoon salad on greens, and accompany with assorted sausages.

6 to 8 servings

Gourmet French Dressing

¾ cup olive oil
¼ cup vinegar (tarragon or cider)
¼ teaspoon Worcestershire sauce
1 clove garlic, cut in halves
1 teaspoon sugar
½ teaspoon salt
¼ teaspoon paprika
¼ teaspoon dry mustard
⅛ teaspoon ground black pepper
⅛ teaspoon ground thyme

1. Combine oil, vinegar, Worcestershire sauce, garlic, sugar, salt, paprika, dry mustard, pepper, and thyme in a jar; cover and shake well. Chill in refrigerator.
2. Before serving, remove garlic and beat or shake dressing thoroughly.

About 1 cup dressing

Roquefort French Dressing: Follow recipe for Gourmet French Dressing. Blend **3 ounces (about ¾ cup) Roquefort cheese,** crumbled, and **2 teaspoons water** until smooth. Add dressing slowly to cheese, blending well.

No-Oil Salad Dressing

½ cup water
½ cup white wine vinegar
1 tablespoon cold water
2 teaspoons cornstarch
1 tablespoon sugar
1 tablespoon chopped parsley
1 teaspoon salt
½ teaspoon basil
¼ teaspoon paprika
¼ teaspoon dry mustard
⅛ teaspoon ground white pepper

1. Heat ½ cup water and vinegar to boiling. Blend 1 tablespoon cold water and cornstarch; pour into vinegar mixture, stirring constantly.
2. Cook and stir until slightly thickened. Stir in sugar, parsley, salt, basil, paprika, dry mustard, and pepper. Chill thoroughly.
3. Serve on tossed salad greens.

About 1 cup dressing

Cooked Salad Dressing

¼ cup sugar
1 tablespoon flour
½ teaspoon dry mustard
½ teaspoon salt
⅛ teaspoon ground pepper
1 cup water
¼ cup cider vinegar
4 egg yolks, fork beaten
2 tablespoons butter or margarine

1. Blend sugar, flour, dry mustard, salt, and pepper in a heavy saucepan. Add water gradually, stirring constantly. Bring rapidly to boiling; cook and stir mixture 2 minutes. Stir in vinegar.
2. Stir about 3 tablespoons of the hot mixture into the beaten egg yolks. Immediately blend into mixture in saucepan. Cook and stir until slightly thickened.
3. Remove from heat and blend in butter. Cool; chill. Store in a covered jar in refrigerator.

About 1½ cups dressing

Creamy Cooked Salad Dressing

2 tablespoons sugar
⅛ teaspoon salt
2 tablespoons cider vinegar
2 tablespoons pineapple syrup
3 egg yolks, slightly beaten
1 tablespoon butter or margarine
1 cup chilled whipping cream, whipped

1. Mix sugar and salt in a heavy saucepan. Stir in vinegar and pineapple syrup. Bring to boiling, stirring constantly.
2. Stir about 2 tablespoons of the hot mixture into egg yolks until blended. Immediately blend into mixture in saucepan. Cook and stir until slightly thickened.
3. Remove from heat; blend in butter. Cool and chill.
4. Blend chilled mixture into whipped cream. Cover and refrigerate until ready to use.

About 2 cups dressing

Gourmet Salad Dressing

3 ounces Roquefort cheese,
   crumbled (about ¾ cup)
1 package (3 ounces) cream
   cheese, softened
1 cup dairy sour cream
⅓ cup sherry
1 tablespoon grated onion
½ teaspoon salt
¼ teaspoon paprika
1 or 2 drops Tabasco

1. Put Roquefort cheese into a bowl. Blend in cream cheese until smooth.
2. Add sour cream, sherry, onion, salt, paprika, and Tabasco; blend until creamy. Store dressing, covered, in refrigerator.

About 2 cups dressing

Enchanting Fruit Dressing

A fitting partner for fruit.

½ cup water
½ cup honey
8 mint leaves
⅛ teaspoon whole cardamom
   seed (contents of 3
   cardamom pods), crushed
¼ teaspoon salt
½ cup sherry, madeira, or port
1 tablespoon lemon juice

1. Put water, honey, mint leaves (bruise the mint with the back of a spoon), and cardamom seed into a small saucepan with a tight-fitting cover. Set over low heat and stir until mixed. Cover saucepan and bring rapidly to boiling. Boil gently 5 minutes. Remove from heat and stir in salt. Set aside to cool.
2. When mixture is cool, strain it and blend in sherry and lemon juice.

About 1⅓ cups dressing

Peach Wine Mold

1 can (29 ounces) sliced peaches
1 package (6 ounces) lemon-
   flavored gelatin
1½ cups boiling water
1 cup white wine
⅓ cup sliced celery
⅓ cup slivered blanched almonds
   Curly endive

1. Drain peaches thoroughly, reserving 1¼ cups syrup. Reserve and refrigerate about 8 peach slices for garnish. Cut remaining peaches into pieces; set aside.
2. Pour gelatin into a bowl, add boiling water, and stir until gelatin is dissolved. Stir in reserved syrup and wine. Chill until partially set.
3. Mix peaches, celery, and almonds into gelatin. Turn into a 1½-quart fancy mold. Chill until firm.
4. Unmold salad onto a serving plate. Garnish with curly endive and reserved peach slices.

About 8 servings

SOUPS

Mulligatawny Soup

Mulligatawny soup is from India, and as you might expect, the distinctive flavor is curry. Curry recipes do not always call for curry powder. The authentic ones call for a combination of spices, such as turmeric, cumin, coriander, dill, and cardamom. This version of mulligatawny calls for both curry powder and several other seasonings.

1 cup diced uncooked chicken (see Note)
¼ cup chopped onion
¼ cup chopped celery
¼ cup diced carrot
2 tart apples, pared and sliced
¼ cup fat or margarine
¼ cup flour
1 teaspoon curry powder
1½ quarts chicken broth
1 tomato, peeled and chopped, or 1 cup drained canned tomatoes, chopped
½ green pepper, minced
1 teaspoon minced parsley
1 teaspoon salt
1 teaspoon sugar
⅛ teaspoon pepper
⅛ teaspoon mace
2 whole cloves
1 cup cooked rice (optional)

1. Cook chicken, onion, celery, carrots, and apple in melted fat in a large saucepan until lightly browned.
2. Stir in flour and curry powder. Gradually add chicken broth, stirring constantly.
3. Stir in remaining ingredients. Cook, covered, over low heat until chicken is tender.
4. Remove and reserve chicken. Strain soup, discarding cloves.
5. Purée vegetables in an electric blender or force through a sieve or food mill. Return soup and vegetable purée to saucepan. Mix in chicken and heat to serving temperature.
6. If desired, mix in hot cooked rice.

8 servings

Note: If making your own chicken broth, substitute the cooked chicken meat for the uncooked chicken and add to soup for final heating.

Greek Egg-Lemon Soup

Lemons are to Greece as oranges are to Florida—they just can't seem to get enough of them. And this soup is as common to them as chicken-noodle is to Americans.

6 cups rich veal or chicken broth or 6 bouillon cubes in 6 cups water
⅓ cup uncooked rice
3 eggs
¼ cup lemon juice

1. Bring broth to boiling in a large saucepan. Add rice; cover and simmer until rice is tender, about 20 minutes.
2. Beat eggs until frothy in a bowl; add lemon juice. Beat in 2 cups of broth very slowly; stir the mixture into the remaining soup.
3. Heat to serving temperature, being very careful not to let it boil (boiling will curdle the egg).

4 to 6 servings

French Onion Soup (Soupe à l'Oignon)

The originator of this famous French soup was King Louis XV, who returned late one night to his hunting lodge and found only onions, butter, and champagne on hand. So hungry and weary was he that he simply mixed them together. Voilà—French Onion Soup! A toasted cheese crouton is traditionally part of the recipe, so there's no need to serve additional bread.

5 medium onions, sliced (4 cups) 3 tablespoons butter or margarine 1½ quarts beef broth ½ teaspoon salt ⅛ teaspoon pepper Cheese Croutons	1. Sauté onions in melted butter in a large saucepan. Cook slowly, stirring until golden (about 10 minutes). 2. Blend in beef broth, salt, and pepper. Bring to boiling, cover, and simmer 15 minutes. 3. Pour soup into warm soup bowls or crocks. Float a cheese crouton in each bowl of soup.

6 servings

Cheese Croutons

6 slices French bread, toasted 2 tablespoons butter or margarine ¼ cup (1 ounce) grated Gruyère or Swiss cheese	1. Spread one side of each bread slice with butter. If necessary, cut bread to fit size of bowl. Sprinkle cheese over buttered toast. 2. Place under broiler until cheese melts.

Hungarian Goulash Soup

The Hungarians use grated potato for a thickening in this soup, with wonderful results.

1½ pounds beef for stew, cut into ½-inch cubes
1 tablespoon shortening or vegetable oil
1 large onion, chopped
1 quart water
¾ cup grated potato (about 1 large)
1 tablespoon paprika
1 tablespoon tomato sauce or ketchup
1 teaspoon salt
½ teaspoon caraway seed (optional)
¼ teaspoon crushed thyme
Pinch red pepper
1 cup chopped pared raw potato (about 1 large)
1 cup uncooked egg noodles

1. Brown meat in shortening in a large saucepan. Add onion; cook until tender.
2. Add water, grated potato, and seasonings. Bring to boiling; cover. Simmer 1½ hours, or until beef is tender.
3. Stir in potatoes and noodles. Cook until tender, 10 to 20 minutes.

4 to 6 servings

Hungarian Goulash Soup with Spaetzle: Follow recipe for Hungarian Goulash Soup, omitting chopped potato and noodles. Serve with **hot buttered spaetzle.**

Spaetzle

2 cups all-purpose flour
1 teaspoon salt
1 egg
¼ to ½ cup water

1. Combine flour and salt; stir in egg. Gradually add water until batter is stiff, but smooth. Place on wet cutting board; flatten.
2. With a wet knife, scrape small pieces of dough off and drop into boiling salted water. Cook only one layer of spaetzle at a time, boiling gently 5 to 8 minutes, or until done. Remove with perforated spoon.

Note: Spaetzle may be served in pea, lentil, or tomato soup or as a side dish, either tossed with hot melted butter or sautéed in butter. For variety, sprinkle with toasted bread crumbs or grated Parmesan cheese.

Baked Minestrone

1½ pounds lean beef for stew, cut
    in 1-inch cubes
1 cup coarsely chopped onion
2 cloves garlic, crushed
1 teaspoon salt
¼ teaspoon pepper
2 tablespoons olive oil
3 cans (about 10 ounces each)
    condensed beef broth
2 soup cans water
1½ teaspoons herb seasoning
1 can (16 ounces) tomatoes
    (undrained)
1 can (15¼ ounces) kidney beans
    (undrained)
1 can (6 ounces) pitted ripe olives
    (undrained)
1½ cups thinly sliced carrots
1 cup small seashell macaroni
2 cups sliced zucchini
    Grated Parmesan cheese

1. Mix beef, onion, garlic, salt, and pepper in a large saucepan. Add olive oil and stir to coat meat evenly.
2. Bake at 400°F 30 minutes, or until meat is browned, stirring occasionally.
3. Turn oven control to 350°F. Add broth, water, and seasonings; stir. Cover; cook 1 hour, or until meat is tender.
4. Stir in tomatoes, kidney beans, olives, carrots, and macaroni. Put sliced zucchini on top. Cover; bake 30 to 40 minutes, or until carrots are tender.
5. Serve with grated cheese.

10 to 12 servings

Lebanon Lentil Soup

2 quarts beef broth
1 ham bone
1¼ cups (about ½ pound) lentils
2 stalks celery, sliced
2 carrots, sliced
1 onion, sliced
1 teaspoon salt
¼ teaspoon pepper
½ teaspoon crushed thyme or ¼
    teaspoon dill weed

1. Combine all ingredients in a large saucepan. Bring to boiling. Cover; simmer 1 to 2 hours, or until lentils are tender.
2. Remove ham bone. Force soup mixture through a coarse sieve or food mill, or purée in an electric blender.
3. Heat, if necessary.

8 servings

Cream of Lentil Soup: Follow recipe for Lebanon Lentil Soup. After puréeing, stir in **1 cup half-and-half** or **whipping cream.**

Bean and Prosciutto Soup

2 cups (about ¾ pound) dried
   beans, soaked overnight
5 cups water
2 cups sliced celery
3 to 4 ounces sliced prosciutto, cut
   in thin strips
1 can (16 ounces) tomatoes
1 can (about 10 ounces) condensed
   beef broth
1 teaspoon salt
1 garlic clove, crushed
2 packages (9 ounces each) frozen
   Italian green beans
3 sprigs fresh parsley, minced
   (about 2 tablespoons)

1. Combine soaked dried beans, water, celery, prosciutto, tomatoes, beef broth, salt, and garlic in a 5-quart saucepot. Bring to boiling; simmer, covered, 30 minutes.
2. Mix in green beans and parsley; simmer 5 to 10 minutes.

10 to 12 servings

Tomato-Lentil Soup

2 cups chopped carrots
1 cup chopped onion
1 cup sliced celery
2 tablespoons margarine, melted
1 clove garlic, crushed
1¼ cups (½ pound) dried lentils
2 quarts water
1 tablespoon salt
1 can (6 ounces) tomato paste
¼ teaspoon crushed dill weed or
   tarragon

1. Sauté carrots, onion, and celery in margarine in a large saucepan until tender.
2. Add garlic, lentils, water, and salt. Simmer 2 hours, or until lentils are tender.
3. Add tomato paste and dill weed; stir.

6 to 8 servings

Farm-Style Leek Soup

2 large leeks (1 pound) with part
   of green tops, sliced
2 medium onions, sliced
1 large garlic clove, minced
¼ cup butter or margarine
4 cups chicken stock or bouillon
2 cups uncooked narrow or
   medium noodles (3 ounces)
1 can or bottle (12 ounces) beer
1½ cups shredded semisoft cheese
   (Muenster, brick, process,
   etc.)
   Salt and pepper

1. Cook leek, onion, and garlic in butter for 15 minutes, using low heat and stirring often.
2. Add stock. Cover and simmer 30 minutes.
3. Add noodles. Cover and simmer 15 minutes, or until noodles are tender.
4. Add beer; heat to simmering. Gradually add cheese, cooking slowly and stirring until melted. Season to taste with salt and pepper.

6 servings, about 1½ cups each

New England Clam Chowder

2 tablespoons butter or margarine
½ cup finely diced celery
¼ cup thinly sliced leek (white part only)
¼ cup minced onion
¼ cup minced green pepper
3 tablespoons flour
1¾ cups milk
1 cup whipping cream or half-and-half
½ cup finely diced potato
12 large hard-shelled clams (to prepare, see Note), or 2 cans (about 7 ounces each) minced clams, drained (reserve liquid)
½ teaspoon salt
⅛ teaspoon thyme
3 drops Tabasco
Pinch white pepper
½ teaspoon Worcestershire sauce
Finely chopped parsley

1. Melt butter over low heat in a heavy 3-quart saucepan. Add celery, leek, onion, and green pepper. Stirring occasionally, cook 6 to 8 minutes, or until partially tender.
2. Blend flour into the vegetable-butter mixture; heat until bubbly. Gradually add milk and cream, stirring constantly. Bring to boiling, stirring constantly; cook 1 to 2 minutes.
3. Stir in potato, reserved clam liquid, salt, thyme, Tabasco, and pepper. Bring to boiling and simmer 25 to 35 minutes, stirring frequently. Add minced clams and Worcestershire sauce.
4. Pour into soup tureen or individual soup bowls. Garnish with parsley.

4 to 6 servings

Note: To prepare clams and broth, rinse clams thoroughly under running cold water. Place clams in saucepan and add 3 cups water. Cook over medium heat until shells open completely. Drain the clams, reserving 2 cups of broth for chowder. Remove clams from shells. Cut off the hard outsides (combs) and chop clams into small, fine pieces. Decrease milk in chowder to 1 cup.

Cream of Broccoli Soup

2 packages (10 ounces each) frozen chopped broccoli
1 cup water
½ cup sliced celery
1 small onion, sliced
2 tablespoons butter or margarine
2 tablespoons flour
1½ quarts chicken stock
2 egg yolks, beaten
½ cup half-and-half or milk
½ teaspoon salt
Pinch pepper
Paprika

1. Cook broccoli in water 3 to 5 minutes; reserve liquid.
2. Sauté celery and onion in butter; stir in flour. Gradually add stock and liquid from broccoli, stirring constantly, until thickened.
3. Add broccoli; put through a food mill or purée in an electric blender, if desired.
4. Stir egg yolks into half-and-half; gradually add to soup, being careful not to boil. Season with salt and pepper.
5. Garnish each serving with a sprinkle of paprika.

6 servings

Chinese Cabbage Soup

2 cups cooked chicken, cut into strips (about 1 chicken breast)
7 cups chicken broth
6 cups sliced Chinese cabbage (celery cabbage)
1 teaspoon soy sauce
1 teaspoon salt
¼ teaspoon pepper

Combine chicken and chicken broth; bring to boiling. Stir in remaining ingredients; cook only 3 to 4 minutes, or just until cabbage is crisp-tender. (Do not overcook.)

6 servings

Note: If desired, lettuce may be substituted for the Chinese cabbage. Reduce cooking time to 1 minute.

Gazpacho Garden Soup

3 large tomatoes, chopped
1 clove garlic, crushed
1 small cucumber, chopped
1 green pepper, chopped
½ cup sliced green onions
¼ cup chopped onion
¼ cup minced parsley
1 teaspoon crushed rosemary
¼ teaspoon crushed basil
½ teaspoon salt
¼ cup olive oil
¼ cup salad oil
2 tablespoons lemon juice
2 cups chicken broth or 3 chicken
    bouillon cubes dissolved in 2
    cups boiling water, then cooled

1. Combine all ingredients except chicken broth in a large bowl. Toss gently.
2. Stir in chicken broth; chill.
3. Serve in chilled bowls with garnishes suggested in Gazpacho.

6 servings

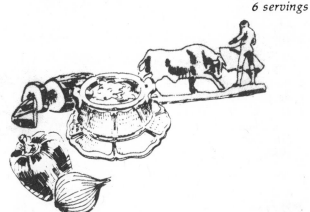

Pioneer Potato Soup

1 quart chicken stock
4 potatoes, chopped (about 4 cups)
2 cups sliced carrots
½ cup sliced celery
¼ cup chopped onion
1 teaspoon salt
½ teaspoon marjoram, dill weed, or
    cumin
⅛ teaspoon white pepper
1 cup milk or half-and-half
2 tablespoons flour
    Garnishes: paprika, sliced green
        onions, crisply cooked
        crumbled bacon, chopped
        pimento, snipped chives or
        parsley, or grated Parmesan
        cheese

1. Combine all ingredients except milk, flour, and garnishes in a large saucepan. Bring to boiling; simmer 30 minutes.
2. Gradually add milk to flour, stirring until smooth. Stir into soup.
3. Bring soup to boiling; boil 1 minute, stirring constantly.
4. Garnish as desired.

4 to 6 servings

Potato Soup with Sour Cream: Follow recipe for Pioneer Potato Soup. Before serving, stir in ½ **cup dairy sour cream.** Heat; do not boil.

Puréed Potato Soup: Follow recipe for either Pioneer Potato or Potato Soup with Sour Cream, omitting the flour. Purée in an electric blender before serving. Reheat, if necessary.

Lettuce Soup

Lettuce need not be relegated only to the salad bowl. Chop it up, stir it into a rich broth, and eat it with some San Francisco Sourdough French Bread

2 tablespoons butter or margarine
2 tablespoons flour
1 can (about 10 ounces) condensed
    chicken broth
1 soup can water
½ small head lettuce, cored and
    coarsely chopped
¼ cup thinly sliced celery
1 tablespoon chopped watercress
    Salt and pepper

1. Melt butter in a saucepot; stir in flour and cook until bubbly.
2. Gradually stir in chicken broth and water; bring to boiling, stirring constantly. Cook 1 minute.
3. Stir in lettuce, celery, and watercress. Season with salt and pepper to taste. Cook until vegetables are crisp-tender, about 5 minutes.

About 3 servings

Lobster-Tomato Cream Soup

When you use lobster, you are really going first class. Serve with a bread equally as classy—French Crescents

2 tablespoons minced onion
¼ cup butter
¼ cup flour
¼ teaspoon salt
  Pinch black pepper
2 cups tomato juice
1 cup half-and-half
½ cup milk
1½ teaspoons Worcestershire sauce
4 drops Tabasco
1 can (about 6 ounces) lobster, drained and cut in pieces
3 tablespoons dry sherry
  Whipped cream

1. Sauté onion in melted butter in a large saucepan. Stir in flour, salt, and pepper. Heat until mixture bubbles.
2. Gradually stir in tomato juice, half-and-half, milk, Worcestershire sauce, and Tabasco. Cook until sauce thickens, stirring constantly.
3. Add lobster, reserving a few pieces for garnish. Heat; do not boil. Stir in sherry.
4. Pour into a tureen or individual soup bowls. Garnish with reserved lobster meat and whipped cream.

6 servings

Crab-Tomato Cream Soup: Follow recipe for Lobster-Tomato Cream Soup, except substitute **1 cup (about 4 ounces) flaked fresh crab meat** for the lobster.

Creamy Shrimp and Avocado Bisque

Seafood and fruit join to make an elegant soup. Serve with bowknot-shaped Dinner Rolls

2 cans (about 10 ounces each) condensed cream of asparagus soup
2 cans (about 10 ounces each) condensed cream of potato soup
1 teaspoon curry powder
2 soup cans milk
2 soup cans half-and-half
2 cups cooked shrimp, cut in pieces (see Note)
1 avocado, peeled and chopped
2 tablespoons minced chives

1. Combine soups and curry in a large, heavy saucepan. Stir in milk and half-and-half. Set over low heat until thoroughly heated, stirring occasionally.
2. Mix in shrimp; heat thoroughly; do not boil.
3. Pour into soup tureen; gently stir in avocado. Sprinkle with chives. Serve at once.

10 servings

Note: When using fresh or fresh-frozen shrimp, shell and devein. To remove the vein, make a shallow cut lengthwise down back of each shrimp. Remove vein with point of knife.

Cool and Creamy Shrimp and Avocado Bisque: Follow recipe for Creamy Shrimp and Avocado Bisque; chill before serving.

Consommé

More than just a clear stock, consommé derives its special flavor from the vegetables used. Egg whites and shells clarify this traditional and elegant appetizer soup.

½ cup coarsely chopped celery leaves
½ cup chopped leek (green part only)
½ cup chopped carrots
¼ cup chopped parsley leaves and stems
2 tomatoes, chopped
3 egg whites
3 egg shells, crushed
2 quarts beef stock

1. Combine ingredients in a heavy 4- or 5-quart saucepot. Bring to boiling. Reduce heat; simmer 20 minutes, uncovered and undisturbed.
2. Pour soup into a sieve lined with a double thickness of dampened cheesecloth which has been placed over a large bowl. Serve hot.

6 servings

Double Consommé: Follow recipe for Consommé, adding **1 pound beef,** cut in pieces, with vegetables. Simmer 45 minutes.

Consommé with Vegetables: Follow recipe for Consommé. After straining, add **1 cup thinly sliced cooked vegetables.** Heat.

Bouillabaisse

Truly a bouillabaisse should be served after you've been fishing all day—so you can include your catch! But when you are buying, select 3 different fish plus seafood. Other possibilities besides those listed here are red snapper and whole clams.

⅔ cup chopped onion
2 leeks, chopped (white part only)
¼ cup olive oil
1 clove garlic, crushed
1 can (16 ounces) tomatoes
1 tablespoon minced parsley
½ bay leaf
½ teaspoon savory
½ teaspoon fennel
⅛ teaspoon saffron
1½ teaspoons salt
¼ teaspoon pepper
1 lobster (1½ to 2 pounds) cleaned and cut up, or 8 lobster tails
1½ pounds bass, boned and cut in 1-inch pieces
1 pound perch, boned and cut in 1-inch pieces
1 pound cod, boned and cut in 1-inch pieces
1 pound fresh shelled deveined shrimp
1 pound sea scallops (fresh or thawed frozen)
1 pint oysters
6 slices French bread, toasted

1. Sauté onion and leeks in olive oil in a large Dutch oven. Stir in garlic, tomatoes, parsley, bay leaf, savory, fennel, saffron, salt, pepper, lobster, and bass, and just enough water to cover (1 to 1½ quarts). Bring to boiling; simmer 10 minutes.
2. Add perch and cod; continue to simmer 10 minutes, or until fish are almost tender.
3. Add shrimp and scallops; cook 5 minutes longer.
4. Meanwhile, drain oysters, reserving liquor. Remove any shell particles. Simmer oysters in liquor in a saucepan 3 minutes, or until edges begin to curl. Add to fish mixture.
5. Line a deep serving dish with toasted bread. Cover with fish and pour sauce in which fish has been cooked over all. Serve at once.

About 8 servings

Note: If desired, substitute 1 cup sherry for 1 cup of the water in step 1.

Vichyssoise (Chilled Leek and Potato Soup)

Surprisingly enough, this is an American soup with a French name. Gourmets will insist that it be made with the white part of leeks. (The rest of us will settle for green onions.) Serve very cold.

4 to 6 leeks
2 tablespoons butter or margarine
4 potatoes, pared and sliced
1 quart chicken broth or 6 chicken bouillon cubes dissolved in 1 quart boiling water
1 cup half-and-half
1 cup chilled whipping cream
Snipped chives

1. Finely slice the white part and about an inch of the green part of each leek to measure about 1 cup.
2. Sauté leeks in butter in a heavy saucepan. Stir in potatoes and broth; bring to boiling. Simmer 40 minutes, or until potatoes are tender.
3. Sieve the cooked vegetables or blend until smooth in an electric blender. Mix in half-and-half; chill thoroughly.
4. Just before serving, stir in whipping cream. Garnish with chives.

8 servings

BREADS

Basic White Bread

5½ to 6 cups flour
2 packages active dry yeast
2 tablespoons sugar
2 teaspoons salt
1 cup milk
1 cup water
2 tablespoons oil
Oil or butter

QUICK MIX METHOD

1. Combine 2 cups flour, yeast, sugar, and salt in a large mixing bowl.
2. Heat milk, water, and 2 tablespoons oil in a saucepan over low heat until very warm (120° to 130°F).
3. Add liquid to flour mixture; beat on high speed of electric mixer until smooth, about 3 minutes. Gradually stir in more flour to make a soft dough.
4. Turn onto lightly floured surface and knead until smooth and elastic (5 to 10 minutes).
5. Cover dough with bowl or pan; let rest 20 minutes.
6. For two loaves, divide dough in half and roll out two 14×7-inch rectangles; for one loaf roll out to 16×8-inch rectangle.
7. Roll up from narrow side, pressing dough into roll at each turn. Press ends to seal and fold under loaf.
8. Place in 2 greased 8×4×2-inch loaf pans or 1 greased 9×5×3-inch loaf pan; brush with oil.
9. Let rise in warm place until double in bulk (30 to 45 minutes).
10. Bake at 400°F 35 to 40 minutes.
11. Remove from pans immediately and brush with oil; cool on wire rack.

One 2-pound loaf
or two 1-pound loaves

CONVENTIONAL METHOD

1. Heat milk, sugar, oil, and salt; cool to lukewarm.
2. In a large bowl, sprinkle yeast in warm water (105° to 115°F); stir until dissolved.
3. Add lukewarm milk mixture and 2 cups flour; beat until smooth.
4. Beat in enough additional flour to make a stiff dough.
5. Turn out onto lightly floured surface; let rest 10 to 15 minutes. Knead until smooth and elastic (8 to 10 minutes).
6. Place in a greased bowl, turning to grease top. Cover; let rise in warm place until double in bulk (about 1 hour).
7. Punch down. Let rest 15 minutes.
8. Follow same shaping and baking instructions as Quick Mix Method.

You'll want to try these flavor variations to the Basic White Bread for something different. Shaping variations are also included.

Cheese Bread: Add **1 cup (4 ounces) shredded Cheddar cheese** before the last portion of the flour.

Onion Bread: Omit the salt and add **1 package (1⅜ ounces) dry onion soup mix** to the warm milk.

Mini Loaves: Divide dough into 10 equal pieces. Shape into loaves. Place in 10 greased 4½×2½×1½-inch loaf pans. Cover; let rise until double in bulk (about 20 minutes). Bake at 350°F 20 to 25 minutes.

Braided Egg Bread: Reduce milk to ½ cup. Add **2 eggs** with warm liquid to the flour mixture. Divide dough into 3 equal pieces. Form each into a rope, 15×12 inches. Braid. Tuck ends under. Place on a greased baking sheet or 9×5×3-inch loaf pan. Cover and let rise and bake the same as basic recipe.

French Bread: Omit the milk and oil and use **2 cups water.** Divide dough in half. Roll each half into 15×12-inch rectangle. Beginning at long side, roll up tightly. Seal seams. Taper the ends. With a sharp knife, make ¼-inch deep diagonal cuts along loaf tops. Cover. Let rise until less than double in bulk (about 20 minutes). Brush with water. Bake at 400°F 15 minutes, then reduce to 350°F and bake 15 to 20 minutes longer. For crisper crust, put pan of hot water in bottom of oven and 5 minutes before loaf is done, brush with glaze of **1 beaten egg white** and **1 tablespoon cold water.**

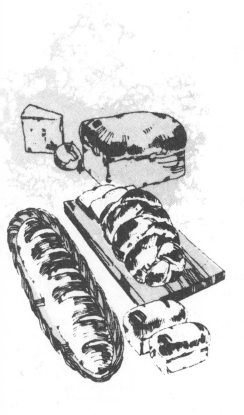

Delicatessen Rye Bread

You'll notice when making rye breads that the dough is stickier and has a different consistency than whole wheat flour doughs.

2 to 2¾ cups all-purpose or
 unbleached flour
2 cups rye flour
2 teaspoons salt
2 packages active dry yeast
1 tablespoon caraway seed
1 cup milk
¾ cup water
2 tablespoons molasses
2 tablespoons oil

1. Combine 1¾ cups all-purpose flour, salt, yeast, and caraway seed in a large mixing bowl.
2. Heat milk, water, molasses, and oil in a saucepan over low heat until very warm (120° to 130°F).
3. Add liquid gradually to flour mixture, beating on high speed of electric mixer; scrape bowl occasionally. Add 1 cup rye flour, or enough to make a thick batter. Beat at high speed 2 minutes. Stir in remaining rye flour and enough all-purpose flour to make a soft dough.
4. Turn dough onto a floured surface; knead until smooth and elastic (about 5 minutes).
5. Cover with bowl or pan and let rest 20 minutes.
6. Divide in half. Shape into 2 round loaves; place on greased baking sheets. Cover; let rise until double in bulk (30 to 45 minutes).
7. Bake at 375°F 35 to 40 minutes, or until done.

2 loaves

Basic Dinner Rolls

4 to 4¾ cups all-purpose flour
2 tablespoons sugar
2 packages active dry yeast
1 teaspoon salt
1 cup milk
½ cup water
¼ cup butter or margarine
1 egg (at room temperature)
Melted butter (optional)

1. Combine 1½ cups flour, sugar, yeast, and salt in a mixing bowl.
2. Heat milk, water, and butter until very warm (120° to 130°F).
3. Add liquid and egg to flour mixture; beat until smooth, about 3 minutes.
4. Stir in enough remaining flour to make a soft, sticky dough.
5. Turn dough onto a floured surface; continue to work in flour until dough can be kneaded. Knead until smooth and elastic, but still soft (about 5 minutes).
6. Cover dough with bowl or pan. Let rest 20 minutes.
7. Shape dough as desired. Cover and let rise until double in bulk (about 15 minutes).
8. Bake at 425°F about 12 minutes. Cool on wire racks. Brush with butter if desired.

2 to 2½ dozen rolls

Pan Rolls: Divide dough into 24 equal pieces by first dividing dough in half and then each half into 12 equal pieces. Roll into balls. Place in a greased 13×9×2-inch baking pan. Brush with melted butter, if desired.

Cloverleaf Rolls: Pinch off bits of dough; roll into 1-inch balls. For each roll, place 3 balls in a greased muffin-pan well.

Crescents: Divide dough in half. Roll each half into a 12-inch round about ¼ inch thick. Brush with **2 tablespoons melted butter.** Cut into 12 wedges. For each crescent, roll up wedge beginning at side opposite the point. Place point-side down on a greased baking sheet; curve ends.

Snails: Roll dough into a rectangle ¼ inch thick. Cut off strips ½ inch wide and 5 inches long. Roll each piece of dough into a rope about 10 inches long. Wind into a flat coil, tucking ends under. Place on greased baking sheet.

Figure Eights: Shape strips of dough ½ inch wide and 5 inches long into 10-inch ropes as in Snails (above). For each roll, pinch ends of rope together and twist once to form a figure 8. Place on greased baking sheets.

Twists: Follow procedure for Figure Eights, giving each 8 an additional twist.

Bowknots: Roll dough into a rectangle ¼ inch thick. Cut off strips ½ inch wide and 5 inches long. Roll each strip into a smooth rope 9 or 10 inches long. Gently tie into a single or double knot. Place on a greased baking sheet.

Parker House Rolls: Roll dough ¼ inch thick. Brush with **3 or 4 tablespoons melted butter.** Cut with a 2½-inch round cutter. With a knife handle, make a crease across each circle slightly off center. Fold larger half over the smaller, pressing edges to seal. Place on a greased baking sheet or close together in a greased 13×9×2-inch baking pan.

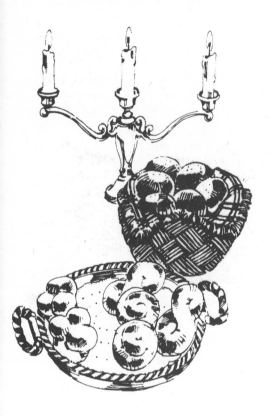

Braids: Form several ropes, ½ inch in diameter. Braid 3 ropes into a long strip; cut into 3-inch lengths. Pinch together at each end. Place on a greased baking sheet.

Butterflies: Divide dough in half. Roll each half into a 24×6-inch rectangle about ¼ inch thick. Brush with **2 tablespoons melted butter.** Starting with long side, roll up dough as for jelly roll. Cut off 2-inch pieces. With handle of knife, press crosswise at center of each roll, forming a deep groove so spiral sides become visible. Place on a greased baking sheet.

Fantans or Butterflake Rolls: Roll dough into a rectangle ¼ inch thick. Brush with **3 or 4 tablespoons melted butter.** Cut into 1-inch strips. Stack 6 or 7 strips; cut each into 1½-inch sections. Place on end in greased muffin-pan wells.

Crusty Hard Rolls

If you like a crunchy roll, try this one. A shiny golden crust surrounds the snowy white and moist interior.

3½ to 4½ cups all-purpose flour
2 packages active dry yeast
1 tablespoon sugar
1½ teaspoons salt
1 cup hot tap water (120° to 130°F)
2 tablespoons vegetable oil
1 egg white
1 egg yolk
1 tablespoon water

1. Combine 1 cup flour, yeast, sugar, and salt in a large mixer bowl. Stir in water, oil, and egg white; beat until smooth, about 3 minutes on high speed of electric mixer. Gradually stir in more flour to make a soft dough.
2. Turn dough onto a floured surface; knead until smooth and elastic (3 to 5 minutes).
3. Cover with bowl or pan and let rest about 20 minutes.
4. Divide into 18 equal pieces. Form each into a smooth oval; place on a greased baking sheet. Slash tops lengthwise about ¼ inch deep. Let rise until double in bulk (about 15 minutes).
5. Brush with a mixture of egg yolk and 1 tablespoon water.
6. Bake at 400°F 15 to 20 minutes. For a crisper crust, place a shallow pan of hot water on lowest oven rack during baking.

1½ dozen rolls

Kaiser Rolls: Follow recipe for Crusty Hard Rolls, only flatten each of the 18 pieces of dough into 4- to 4-½-inch rounds. For each roll, lift one edge of the round and press it into center of circle. Then lift the corner of the fold and press it into the center. Continue clockwise around the circle until 5 or 6 folds have been made. Let rise and bake as directed above.

Sourdough puts a little bit of history in your loaf pan. About 6,000 years ago the Egyptians accidentally discovered that when flour was exposed to water and the wild yeast in the air, it fermented and expanded. When the fermented dough was added to bread dough, the result was a lighter bread. The "starter" was passed down from generation to generation to produce the staff of life for thousands of years.

In this country, gold prospectors carried the starter with them everywhere they went, and soon they themselves became known as Sourdoughs.

Sourdough requires a little know-how in order to nurture it and see that it performs as expected. Read these helpful hints to guide you in making sourdough breads.

Hints: Use your starter often. Don't let it become tucked away in the back of the refrigerator where you'll forget about it. Sourdough that is allowed to sit unused for 2 or 3 months will spoil and have to be discarded.

If you have replenished the starter, make sure that you wait at least 8 hours before using it.

The old sourdoughs, the name given to prospectors who always carried the sourdough starter with them, referred to the process of replenishing the starter as "sweetening" it. When replenishing, use warm water (105° to 115°F) to provide the best environment for yeast growth. Just as packaged yeast is vulnerable to too high temperatures, so is the yeast in sourdough starters.

Store your starter in the refrigerator. You may want to keep as much as 2 cups on hand so you'll be ready either for quantity baking or for sharing with a friend.

Sourdough Starter

2 cups flour
1 package active dry yeast
1 tablespoon sugar
2 cups warm potato water (105° to 115°F)

1. Combine flour, yeast, and sugar in a nonmetal mixing bowl. Stir in potato water.
2. Cover; let stand in a warm place (80° to 85°F) for 48 hours.
3. Store in covered jar in refrigerator.

To use in recipe: Stir well before use. Pour out required amount called for in recipe and use as directed.

To replenish remaining starter: Mix in 1 cup each flour and warm water until smooth. Let stand in warm place a few hours until it bubbles again before covering and replacing in refrigerator.

Note: Use in recipe or remove 1 cup starter and replenish every week.

Sourdough Sam's Skillet Loaves

Sourdough and an iron skillet will carry you back to the early prospecting days. For authenticity and mighty good eating, serve it with honey and butter.

1 cup sourdough starter
2½ cups warm water
2 tablespoons honey or sugar
7 to 7½ cups all-purpose flour
¼ cup vegetable oil
1 tablespoon salt
1 teaspoon baking soda
6 tablespoons butter
4 tablespoons cornmeal

1. Combine starter, water, honey, and 5 cups flour in a large nonmetal mixing bowl. Cover with plastic wrap or a wet towel; let stand at room temperature 12 hours or overnight.
2. Stir in oil. Combine salt, soda, and 1 cup flour. Stir into dough; beat until smooth.
3. Stir in enough remaining flour to make a soft dough.
4. Turn dough onto a floured surface; continue to work in flour until dough is stiff enough to knead. Knead until smooth and elastic (about 5 minutes).
5. Divide dough in half. Roll each into a 10-inch round (see Note).
6. For each loaf, melt 3 tablespoons butter in a heavy 10-inch cast-iron skillet with heat-resistant handle. Sprinkle with 2 tablespoons cornmeal. Place dough in skillet. Turn over to coat top with butter and cornmeal. Let rise 15 minutes.
7. Bake at 400°F 25 to 30 minutes, or until done.
8. Serve hot with **butter** and **honey**.

2 loaves

Note: If you don't have 2 skillets, simply allow the second dough circle to rise while the first bakes—it will just have a lighter texture.

Sweet and Sourdough Granola Bread:
Prepare dough as in Sourdough Sam's Skillet Loaves. After dividing dough in half, roll out each half into a 16×6-inch rectangle. Brush each with **2 tablespoons melted butter** and sprinkle with half the Granola Cinnamon Filling. Beginning with narrow end of rectangle, roll up tightly as for jelly roll; seal edges. Place loaves in 2 greased 9×5×3-inch loaf pans. Cover; let rise until double in bulk (45 to 60 minutes). Bake at 350°F 40 to 45 minutes.

Granola Cinnamon Filling: Combine **1 cup granola**, ½ cup firmly packed brown sugar, ½ cup chopped dates or raisins (optional), and 1 teaspoon cinnamon.

Sourdough Apple Kuchen:
Prepare dough as in Sourdough Sam's Skillet Loaves. After dividing dough, roll out each half into a 10-inch round. Place dough in 2 greased 9- or 10-inch springform pans. Press dough about 1½ inches up sides of pan. Fill each kuchen with a mixture of **2 cups finely sliced pared apples, ½ cup firmly packed brown sugar, ¼ cup all-purpose flour, and 1 teaspoon cinnamon.** Sprinkle with ¼ cup sliced almonds. Dot with **2 tablespoons butter.** Let rise 30 minutes. Bake at 375°F 40 to 45 minutes, or until done.

San Francisco Sourdough French Bread

1 cup sourdough starter
1½ cups warm water
2 tablespoons sugar
5 to 6 cups all-purpose flour
1 tablespoon salt
½ teaspoon baking soda

1. Combine starter, water, sugar, and 3 cups flour in a large nonmetal mixing bowl. Cover with plastic wrap or a towel; let stand at room temperature 12 hours or overnight.
2. Combine salt, soda, and 1 cup flour. Stir into dough; beat until smooth.
3. Stir in enough remaining flour to make a soft dough.
4. Turn dough onto a floured surface; continue to work in flour until dough is stiff enough to knead. Knead until smooth and elastic (5 to 8 minutes).
5. Shape dough into a long, narrow loaf by rolling and stretching dough as for French Bread (page 15). Place on a greased baking sheet. Cover; let rise in a warm place until double in bulk (1½ to 2 hours).
6. With a sharp knife, slash top ½ inch deep at 2-inch intervals. Brush loaf with **water.**
7. Bake at 375°F 30 to 35 minutes.

1 loaf

Note: For a browner and shinier crust, brush before baking with a mixture of **1 egg white** and **⅓ cup water** instead of only water.

Peasant Black Bread

3½ cups rye flour
½ cup unsweetened cocoa
¼ cup sugar
3 tablespoons caraway seed
2 packages active dry yeast
1 tablespoon instant coffee
  (powder or crystals)
2 teaspoons salt
2½ cups hot water (120°-130°F)
¼ cup vinegar
¼ cup dark molasses
¼ cup vegetable oil or melted
  butter
3½ to 4½ cups unbleached or
  all-purpose flour

1. Thoroughly mix rye flour, cocoa, sugar, caraway, yeast, coffee, and salt in a large mixing bowl.
2. Stir in water, vinegar, molasses, and oil; beat until smooth.
3. Stir in enough unbleached flour to make a soft dough.
4. Turn onto a floured surface. Knead until smooth and elastic (about 5 minutes).
5. Place in an oiled bowl; turn to oil top of dough. Cover; let rise in warm place until doubled (about 1 hour).
6. Punch dough down. Divide in half; shape each half into a ball and place in center of 2 greased 8-inch round cake pans. Cover; let rise until double in bulk (about 1 hour).
7. Bake at 350°F 40 to 45 minutes, or until done.

2 loaves

PASTA & GRAINS

Lemony Meat Sauce with Spaghetti

2 pounds ground beef
1½ cups finely chopped onion
1¼ cups chopped green pepper
2 cloves garlic, minced
¼ cup firmly packed brown sugar
1 teaspoon salt
¼ teaspoon ground black pepper
1 teaspoon thyme, crushed
½ teaspoon basil, crushed
2 cups water
2 cans (8 ounces each) tomato sauce
2 cans (6 ounces each) tomato paste
1 can (6 ounces) sliced broiled
   mushrooms (undrained)
1 tablespoon grated lemon peel
¼ cup lemon juice
1 pound enriched spaghetti
   Shredded Parmesan cheese

1. Put meat, onion, green pepper, and garlic into a heated large heavy saucepot or Dutch oven. Cook 10 to 15 minutes, cutting meat apart with fork or spoon.
2. Stir in brown sugar, salt, pepper, thyme, basil, water, tomato sauce, and tomato paste. Cover and simmer 2 to 3 hours, stirring occasionally. About 30 minutes before serving, mix in mushrooms with liquid and lemon peel and juice.
3. Meanwhile, cook spaghetti following package directions; drain.
4. Spoon sauce over hot spaghetti and sprinkle generously with cheese.

10 to 12 servings

Polenta

2 tablespoons olive oil
1 clove garlic, crushed
1 can (8 ounces) sliced mushrooms,
   drained, or 1 pound fresh
   mushrooms, sliced
1 can (16 ounces) tomatoes
   (undrained)
⅓ cup tomato paste
1 teaspoon salt
¼ teaspoon ground pepper
3 cups water
1½ teaspoons salt
1 cup enriched cornmeal
1 cup cold water
   Grated Parmesan or Romano
   cheese

1. Heat olive oil and garlic in a skillet. Add mushrooms and cook about 5 minutes, stirring occasionally. When lightly browned, stir in tomatoes with liquid, tomato paste, salt, and pepper. Simmer 15 to 20 minutes.
2. Meanwhile, bring 3 cups water and 1½ teaspoons salt to boiling in a saucepan. Mix cornmeal and 1 cup cold water; stir into boiling water. Continue boiling, stirring constantly to prevent sticking, until mixture is thick. Cover, reduce heat, and cook over low heat 10 minutes or longer.
3. Turn cooked cornmeal onto warm serving platter and top with the tomato-mushroom mixture. Sprinkle with grated cheese. Serve at once.

6 to 8 servings

White Clam Sauce for Linguine

12 ounces enriched linguine
¼ cup olive oil
½ cup chopped onion
¼ cup snipped parsley
3 cloves garlic, minced
2 tablespoons flour
¼ to ½ teaspoon salt
Few grains pepper
3 cans (8 ounces each) minced clams, drained; reserve 1½ cups liquid

1. Cook linguine following package directions; drain and keep hot.
2. Meanwhile, heat oil in a large skillet. Add onion, parsley, and garlic; cook about 3 minutes, stirring occasionally.
3. Mix in flour, salt, and pepper; cook until bubbly. Add reserved clam liquid gradually, while blending thoroughly. Bring rapidly to boiling, stirring constantly, and boil 1 to 2 minutes. Mix in the minced clams and heat; do not boil.
4. Serve clam sauce on the hot linguine.

6 servings

Rice Pilaf Deluxe

⅓ cup butter
1½ cups uncooked enriched white rice
⅓ cup chopped onion
1½ teaspoons salt
3 cans (13¾ ounces each) chicken broth
¾ cup golden raisins
3 tablespoons butter
¾ cup coarsely chopped pecans
½ teaspoon salt

1. Heat ⅓ cup butter in a heavy skillet. Add rice and onion and cook until lightly browned, stirring frequently.
2. Add 1½ teaspoons salt, chicken broth, and raisins; cover, bring to boiling, reduce heat, and simmer until rice is tender and liquid is absorbed (20 to 25 minutes).
3. Just before serving, heat 3 tablespoons butter in a small skillet. Add pecans and ½ teaspoon salt; heat 2 to 3 minutes, stirring occasionally.
4. Serve rice topped with salted pecans.

About 8 servings

Spanish Rice au Gratin

½ cup uncooked enriched white rice
1 cup water
½ teaspoon salt
1½ tablespoons butter or margarine
½ cup chopped onion
½ cup chopped celery
⅓ cup chopped green pepper
1 cup canned tomatoes, cut in pieces
½ teaspoon salt
½ teaspoon monosodium glutamate
1 teaspoon sugar
¾ teaspoon chili powder
¼ teaspoon Worcestershire sauce
1 cup (about 4 ounces) shredded Cheddar cheese

1. Combine rice, water, and ½ teaspoon salt in a saucepan. Bring to boiling, reduce heat, and simmer, covered, about 14 minutes.
2. Meanwhile, heat butter in a skillet. Mix in onion, celery, and green pepper. Cook until vegetables are tender. Mix in cooked rice, tomatoes, ½ teaspoon salt, monosodium glutamate, sugar, chili powder, and Worcestershire sauce. Simmer until thick.
3. Turn mixture into a greased baking dish. Top evenly with cheese.
4. Place under broiler 3 to 4 inches from heat until cheese is melted.

3 or 4 servings

Mushroom-Rice Casserole

1 cup uncooked white rice
½ cup slivered almonds
1 small onion, chopped
1 can (4 ounces) sliced mushrooms, drained*
¼ cup butter or margarine
2 cups water
2 chicken bouillon cubes
2 tablespoons lemon juice
1 teaspoon soy sauce
    Dash pepper
4 bacon slices, cooked and crumbled
2 tablespoons snipped parsley

1. Sauté rice, almonds, onion, and mushrooms in butter in a skillet. Stir in water, bouillon cubes, lemon juice, soy sauce, and pepper.
2. Heat to boiling. Cover and reduce heat to low. Cook until liquid is absorbed (about 20 minutes).
3. Stir in crumbled bacon and parsley. Put into a 1½-quart casserole.
4. Bake, covered, at 325°F 20 minutes, or until heated through.

6 servings

* The drained mushroom liquid can be used as part of the 2 cups water called for in the recipe.

Italian Rice Casserole

½ cup chopped onion
2 tablespoons oil
1 cup (4 ounces) shredded Cheddar cheese
1 cup sliced fresh mushrooms
¾ cup sliced pitted ripe olives
1 can (16 ounces) stewed tomatoes
1½ cups boiling water
1 package (6 ounces) long-grain and wild rice mix

1. Sauté onion in oil in a skillet. Combine with remaining ingredients. Put into a 2-quart baking dish.
2. Bake, covered, at 350°F 1 hour, or until rice is tender.

6 servings

Rice Loaf

2 cups cooked brown rice
½ cup finely chopped onion
½ cup finely chopped pecans
2 tablespoons snipped parsley
½ teaspoon salt
¼ teaspoon thyme
½ cup milk
1 egg, well beaten

1. Combine all ingredients. Put into a 1-quart casserole.
2. Bake, uncovered, at 350°F 35 to 40 minutes, or until set.

6 servings

Brunch Pilaf

1 package (6 ounces) long-grain and
    wild rice mix
½ pound pork sausage links, cut in
    1-inch pieces
½ pound fresh mushrooms, sliced
3 tablespoons butter or margarine
½ teaspoon salt
¼ teaspoon pepper
2 teaspoons instant minced onion
½ pound chicken livers, cut up

1. Prepare rice according to package directions.
2. Brown sausage in a skillet about 15 minutes. Drain and set aside.
3. Sauté mushrooms in 2 tablespoons butter. Toss with ¼ teaspoon salt, pepper, and minced onion; set aside.
4. Sauté chicken livers in remaining 1 tablespoon butter until lightly browned. Sprinkle with remaining ¼ teaspoon salt.
5. Combine all ingredients and put into a 1½-quart casserole.
6. Bake, covered, at 325°F 30 minutes, or until heated through.

6 to 8 servings

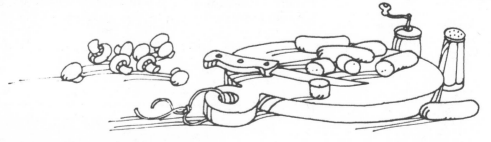

Mushroom Wild Rice

1 package (4 ounces) wild rice
1 medium green pepper, chopped
1 large onion, chopped
½ cup chopped celery
¼ cup butter or margarine
1 egg, beaten
1 can (10¾ ounces) condensed cream
    of mushroom soup
¼ cup sliced almonds
2 tablespoons snipped parsley

1. Prepare rice according to package directions.
2. Sauté green pepper, onion, and celery in butter in a skillet. Add to rice along with beaten egg. Put into a greased 1½-quart casserole.
3. Top with mushroom soup; mix slightly. Sprinkle with almonds.
4. Bake, covered, at 350°F 30 minutes, or until heated through. Sprinkle with parsley.

6 servings

Wild Rice Casserole

1 cup wild rice
2 tablespoons chopped onion
½ pound fresh mushrooms, sliced
½ cup butter or margarine
3 cups broth*
1 teaspoon salt
½ cup toasted slivered almonds

1. Sauté rice, onion, and mushrooms in butter in a skillet. Add broth and salt. Pour into a 1½-quart casserole.
2. Bake, covered, at 325°F 1 hour. Remove cover; top with almonds. Bake an additional 15 minutes, or until rice is tender. If desired, top with fresh tomato wedges.

6 servings

* Use beef broth when serving with meat and chicken broth when serving with poultry.

Farm-Style Leek Soup 17
Peasant Black Bread 28

Petits Pois (New Peas) in Rice Ring

1 package (6 or 6¾ ounces)
 seasoned wild and white rice mix
3 pounds fresh peas
 Butter

1. Cook rice mix according to package directions.
2. Meanwhile, rinse and shell peas just before cooking to retain their delicate flavor. Cook covered in boiling salted water to cover for 15 to 20 minutes or until peas are tender. Drain and add just enough butter so peas glisten.
3. Butter a 1-quart ring mold. When rice is done, turn into the mold, packing down gently with spoon. Invert onto a warm serving platter and lift off mold.
4. Spoon hot peas into center of rice ring just before serving.

About 6 servings

Noodles au Gratin

1 small onion, chopped
¼ cup butter or margarine
4 cups noodles, cooked and drained
½ cup dairy sour cream
6 slices (1 ounce each) American
 cheese, cut in pieces
½ teaspoon salt
½ cup milk
 Paprika

1. Sauté onion in butter in a skillet. Combine with noodles, sour cream, cheese, and salt. Put into a 1½-quart casserole.
2. Pour milk over all. Sprinkle with paprika.
3. Bake, covered, at 350°F 40 minutes, or until golden brown.

6 to 8 servings

Noodles Romanoff

4 cups noodles, cooked and drained
1½ cups (12 ounces) cream-style
 cottage cheese
1 cup dairy sour cream
¼ cup finely chopped onion
1 teaspoon Worcestershire sauce
½ teaspoon salt
¼ teaspoon white pepper
½ cup (2 ounces) shredded Cheddar
 cheese
2 tablespoons snipped parsley

1. Combine all ingredients, except Cheddar cheese and parsley. Put into a 2-quart casserole. Sprinkle with cheese.
2. Bake, covered, at 325°F 40 minutes, or until heated through. Sprinkle with parsley.

6 servings

Roast Leg of Lamb with Spicy Wine Sauce 45
Peach Wine Mold 13

Spaghetti Fromaggi

¼ cup chopped onion
¼ cup chopped green pepper
¼ cup butter or margarine
¼ cup flour
1 teaspoon salt
¼ teaspoon pepper
3½ cups milk
1 cup (4 ounces) shredded Swiss
     cheese
1 cup (4 ounces) shredded Cheddar
     cheese
1 tablespoon Worcestershire sauce
1 tablespoon chopped pimento
1 package (16 ounces) spaghetti,
     cooked and drained
1 tablespoon snipped parsley

1. Sauté onion and green pepper in butter in a skillet. Stir in flour, salt, and pepper. Gradually add milk, stirring until thickened and smooth.
2. Stir in cheeses, Worcestershire sauce, pimento, and spaghetti. Put into a 3-quart casserole.
3. Bake, covered, at 350°F 45 minutes, or until heated through. Sprinkle with parsley.

8 servings

Barley Italienne

6 bacon slices, cut in 1-inch pieces
1½ cups quick-cooking barley
2¼ cups water
1 can (16 ounces) tomatoes
     (undrained)
1 can (8 ounces) tomato sauce
1 medium onion, sliced
1 garlic clove, minced
2 teaspoons salt
½ teaspoon oregano
¼ teaspoon pepper
8 ounces American cheese, sliced

1. Fry bacon in a skillet; drain off excess fat, reserving 2 table-spoons drippings.
2. Brown barley in bacon drippings in skillet. Add water and tomatoes. Bring to a boil; reduce heat. Cover and simmer 10 to 12 minutes, stirring occasionally.
3. Add bacon and remaining ingredients, except cheese. Cover and cook an additional 5 minutes.
4. Layer barley mixture and cheese alternately in a greased 2-quart casserole, ending with cheese on top.
5. Bake, covered, at 350°F 10 to 12 minutes, or until cheese is melted and mixture is heated through.

6 servings

Barley-Mushroom Casserole

½ cup finely chopped onion
½ pound fresh mushrooms, sliced
¼ cup butter or margarine
2 beef bouillon cubes
1 quart boiling water
1 teaspoon salt
1 cup barley

1. Sauté onion and mushrooms in butter in a skillet.
2. Dissolve bouillon cubes in boiling water. Mix with salt, barley, onion, and mushrooms. Pour into a 2-quart casserole.
3. Bake, uncovered, at 350°F 1 hour, stirring occasionally. Cover and bake an additional 30 minutes, or until barley is tender.

6 servings

VEGETABLES

Butter-Sauced Asparagus

2 pounds fresh asparagus, washed,
    or 2 packages (10 ounces each)
    frozen asparagus spears, cooked
¼ cup butter
¼ cup chopped pecans
¼ cup finely chopped celery
1 tablespoon lemon juice

1. Put fresh asparagus into a small amount of boiling salted water in a skillet, bring to boiling, reduce heat, and cook 5 minutes, uncovered; cover and cook 10 minutes, or until just tender.

2. Meanwhile, heat butter in a small saucepan. Add pecans and celery and cook 5 minutes. Stir in lemon juice. Pour over asparagus and serve immediately.

About 6 servings

Broccoli with Buttery Lemon Crunch

1½ pounds broccoli, washed
¼ cup butter or margarine
½ cup coarse dry enriched bread
    crumbs
1 tablespoon grated lemon peel
3 tablespoons butter or margarine
1 small clove garlic, crushed in a
    garlic press or minced
½ teaspoon salt
    Few grains black pepper

1. Cook broccoli in a small amount of boiling salted water until just tender. (Cook uncovered 5 minutes, then cover and cook 10 to 15 minutes, or cook, covered, the full time and lift the lid 3 or 4 times during cooking.)

2. Meanwhile, heat ¼ cup butter in a large skillet; add bread crumbs and heat, stirring frequently, until well browned. Remove crumbs from butter with a slotted spoon and mix with the lemon peel.

3. Put 3 tablespoons butter, garlic, salt, and pepper into skillet; heat until butter is lightly browned. Add broccoli and turn gently until well coated with butter.

4. Arrange broccoli in a heated vegetable dish and pour remaining garlic butter over it. Top with the "lemoned" crumbs.

About 6 servings

Brussels Sprouts in Herb Butter

2 pounds fresh Brussels sprouts
⅓ cup butter
1 tablespoon grated onion
1 tablespoon lemon juice
¾ teaspoon salt
¼ teaspoon thyme
¼ teaspoon marjoram
¼ teaspoon savory

1. Cook Brussels sprouts in boiling salted water until just tender.

2. Put butter, onion, lemon juice, salt, thyme, marjoram, and savory into a saucepan. Set over low heat until butter is melted, stirring to blend.

3. When Brussels sprouts are tender, drain thoroughly and turn into a warm serving dish. Pour the seasoned butter mixture over the Brussels sprouts and toss gently to coat sprouts evenly and thoroughly.

About 8 servings

Zesty Beets

1 can or jar (16 ounces) small whole
  beets
2 tablespoons butter or margarine
2 tablespoons prepared horseradish
½ teaspoon prepared mustard
½ teaspoon seasoned salt

Heat beets in liquid; drain. Add butter, horseradish, prepared mustard, and seasoned salt; stir gently.

About 4 servings

Cabbage Rolls Paprikash

8 large cabbage leaves
2½ cups diced cooked chicken
2 tablespoons chopped onion
½ cup finely chopped celery
¼ pound chopped fresh mushrooms
1 small clove garlic, minced
½ teaspoon salt
½ teaspoon thyme leaves
1 egg, beaten
2 tablespoons butter or margarine
6 tablespoons flour
2 cups chicken broth
2 cups dairy sour cream
3 tablespoons paprika

1. Cook cabbage leaves 4 minutes in boiling salted water to cover. Drain and pat dry.
2. Mix chicken, onion, celery, mushrooms, garlic, salt, and thyme; stir in egg.
3. Place ½ cup of the chicken mixture in the center of each cabbage leaf. Fold sides of the cabbage leaf toward center, over filling, and then fold and overlap ends to make a small bundle. Fasten with wooden picks. Place in a 3-quart baking dish.
4. Heat butter in a large skillet. Blend in flour and heat until bubbly. Add chicken broth gradually, stirring until smooth. Blend in sour cream and paprika. Cook over low heat, stirring constantly, until thickened. Pour sauce over cabbage rolls. Cover baking dish.
5. Cook in a 350°F oven 35 minutes.

4 servings

Cauliflower Italiana

2 packages (10 ounces each) frozen
  cauliflower
2 tablespoons butter or margarine
½ clove garlic, minced
2 teaspoons flour
1 teaspoon salt
1 can (16 ounces) tomatoes
  (undrained)
1 small green pepper, coarsely
  chopped
¼ teaspoon oregano

1. Cook cauliflower following package directions; drain.
2. Meanwhile, heat butter with garlic in a saucepan. Stir in flour and salt and cook until bubbly.
3. Add tomatoes with liquid and bring to boiling, stirring constantly; cook 1 to 2 minutes. Stir in green pepper and oregano.
4. Pour hot sauce over cooked cauliflower.

About 6 servings

Gingered Turnips

Oriental seasonings give this often neglected vegetable new flavor appeal.

2 pounds yellow turnips, pared
  and cubed
1 tablespoon minced onion
1¼ cups Beef Stock
½ teaspoon ground ginger
½ teaspoon sugar
2 teaspoons soy sauce

Combine all ingredients in a saucepan; simmer covered until turnips are tender (about 15 minutes). Drain; mash turnips with potato masher or electric mixer until fluffy, adding cooking liquid as needed for desired consistency.

6 servings

Parsley-Buttered New Potatoes

18 small new potatoes
  Boiling water
1½ teaspoons salt
2 tablespoons butter
1 tablespoon snipped parsley

Scrub potatoes and put into a saucepan. Pour in boiling water to a 1-inch depth. Add salt; cover and cook about 15 minutes, or until tender. Drain and peel. Return potatoes to saucepan and toss with butter and parsley.

About 6 servings

Lacy French-Fried Onion Rings

1 cup enriched all-purpose flour
1 teaspoon baking powder
¼ teaspoon salt
1 egg, well beaten
1 cup milk
1 tablespoon vegetable oil
4 sweet Spanish onions
  Fat for deep frying heated to 375°F
  Salt or garlic salt

1. Blend flour, baking powder, and salt.
2. Combine egg, milk, and oil in a bowl and beat until thoroughly blended. Beat in the dry ingredients until batter is smooth. Cover.
3. Cut off root ends of onions; slip off the loose skins. Slice onions ¼ inch thick and separate into rings.
4. Using a long-handled two-tined fork, immerse a few onion rings at a time into the batter, lift out and drain over bowl a few seconds before dropping into heated fat. Turn only once as they brown; do not crowd.
5. When rings are golden brown on both sides, lift out and drain on absorbent paper-lined cookie sheet. Sprinkle with salt and serve hot.

About 6 servings

Lacy Cornmeal Onion Rings: Follow recipe for Lacy French-Fried Onion Rings. Substitute ½ **cup enriched cornmeal** for ⅔ cup flour.

To Freeze French-Fried Onions: Leaving the crisp, tender rings on the absorbent paper-lined cookie sheet on which they were drained, place in freezer and freeze quickly. Then carefully remove rings to moisture-vaporproof containers with layers of absorbent paper between each layer of onions; the rings may overlap some. Cover tightly, label, and freeze.

To Reheat Frozen French-Fried Onions: Removing the desired number of onion rings, arrange them (frozen) in a single layer on a cookie sheet. Heat in a 375°F oven several minutes, or until rings are crisp and hot.

Turnip Custard

2 pounds turnips
1 egg, well beaten
¼ cup finely crushed soda crackers
⅔ cup (6-ounce can) undiluted
  evaporated milk
1 teaspoon salt
  Few grains black pepper
1 cup (about 4 ounces) shredded
  sharp Cheddar cheese

1. Wash, pare, and cut turnips into pieces. Cook, uncovered, in boiling water to cover until turnips are tender, 15 to 20 minutes; drain. Mash and, if necessary, again drain turnips (about 2 cups mashed turnips).
2. Blend mashed turnips, egg, cracker crumbs, evaporated milk, salt, and pepper. Turn mixture into a buttered 1¼-quart baking dish. Set dish in a pan and pour in boiling water to a 1-inch depth.
3. Bake at 350°F 15 minutes. Sprinkle cheese over top. Bake 5 minutes, or until a knife inserted halfway between center and edge comes out clean. Remove from water immediately.

About 6 servings

Vegetable Salad with Yogurt Dressing

Vivid colors dominate this unusual salad combination.

¾ cup Low-Fat Yogurt
2 tablespoons snipped parsley
½ cup finely chopped dill pickle
½ cup chopped tomato
1 teaspoon salt
1 cup sliced radishes
1 medium zucchini, shredded
2 medium carrots, shredded
1 large beet, shredded

1. Mix yogurt, parsley, pickle, chopped tomato, and salt; refrigerate covered 1 hour.
2. Arrange radish slices around edge of a serving plate. Arrange zucchini, carrots, and beet decoratively in center of plate. Serve yogurt mixture with salad.

4 servings

Layered Casserole

1 can (14½ ounces) asparagus spears, drained
1 can (17 ounces) green peas
1 can (8½ ounces) water chestnuts, drained and sliced
2 tablespoons chopped pimento
½ cup fine dry bread crumbs
1 can (10¾ ounces) condensed cream of mushroom soup
½ cup (2 ounces) shredded American cheese

1. Arrange asparagus spears in bottom of a 1½-quart shallow baking dish.
2. Drain peas, reserving ¼ cup liquid. Top asparagus spears with peas, water chestnuts, and pimento. Sprinkle with ¼ cup bread crumbs.
3. Combine soup with reserved ¼ cup pea liquid. Evenly spread over bread crumbs. Sprinkle with remaining ¼ cup bread crumbs and cheese.
4. Bake, uncovered, at 350°F 20 minutes, or until heated through.

6 servings

Marinated Artichoke Hearts Supreme

2 jars (6 ounces each) marinated artichoke hearts
1 garlic clove, minced
½ cup chopped onion
4 eggs, beaten
¼ cup fine dry bread crumbs
2 tablespoons snipped parsley
½ teaspoon salt
½ teaspoon oregano
¼ teaspoon pepper
¼ teaspoon Tabasco
2 cups (8 ounces) shredded Cheddar cheese

1. Cut up artichoke hearts, reserving liquid from 1 jar.
2. Pour liquid into a skillet and sauté garlic and onion.
3. Combine with eggs, bread crumbs, parsley, salt, oregano, pepper, and Tabasco. Stir in cheese and artichoke hearts. Pour into a greased 1½-quart shallow baking dish.
4. Bake, uncovered, at 325°F 30 minutes, or until set.

6 servings

Broccoli Bake

2 packages (10 ounces each) frozen
chopped broccoli, cooked and
drained
1 can (10¾ ounces) condensed cream
of mushroom soup
½ cup mayonnaise
1 cup (4 ounces) shredded Cheddar
cheese
1 tablespoon lemon juice
½ cup crumbled cheese crackers

1. Spread broccoli in bottom of 10x6-inch baking dish.
2. Combine soup, mayonnaise, cheese, and lemon juice. Spread over broccoli. Sprinkle with cracker crumbs.
3. Bake, uncovered, at 350°F 30 minutes, or until heated through.

6 servings

Broccoli-Mushroom Casserole

1 package (10 ounces) frozen chopped
broccoli, cooked and drained
1 can (4 ounces) mushroom slices,
drained
2 tablespoons chopped pimento
⅓ cup dairy sour cream
½ cup chopped celery
½ teaspoon salt
Dash pepper

1. Combine all ingredients. Put into a 1-quart casserole.
2. Bake, covered, at 350°F 25 minutes, or until heated through.

3 servings

Brussels Sprouts in Broth

2 packages (10 ounces each) frozen
Brussels sprouts, cooked and
drained
1 cup water
1 beef bouillon cube
2 tablespoons butter or margarine
½ cup (2 ounces) freshly grated
Parmesan cheese

1. Put Brussels sprouts into a 1-quart casserole.
2. Heat together water, bouillon cube, and butter. Pour over Brussels sprouts. Sprinkle with cheese.
3. Bake, covered, at 325°F 20 minutes, or until heated through.

6 servings

Note: To improve flavor, cover and refrigerate Brussels sprouts, broth, and butter overnight. Add cheese before baking.

Cabbage Casserole

1 head cabbage, cut in 6 wedges
1½ cups (6 ounces) shredded Cheddar cheese
¼ cup butter or margarine
¼ cup flour
½ teaspoon seasoned salt
½ teaspoon sugar
⅛ teaspoon garlic powder
1¾ cups milk

1. Cook cabbage in **boiling salted water** about 10 minutes, or until tender.
2. Layer cabbage and 1 cup cheese in a 2-quart casserole.
3. Melt butter in a saucepan. Stir in flour, seasoned salt, sugar, and garlic powder. Gradually add milk, stirring until thickened and smooth.
4. Pour over cabbage. Sprinkle with remaining ½ cup cheese.
5. Bake, covered, at 350°F 20 minutes, or until heated through. If desired, sprinkle with paprika.

6 servings

Sour Red Cabbage

1 head red cabbage, shredded
1 onion, finely chopped
2 cooking apples, cored and cut up
¼ cup red wine vinegar
¼ cup water
1 tablespoon firmly packed brown sugar
1 teaspoon salt
¼ teaspoon pepper
1 tablespoon butter

1. Combine all ingredients, except butter.
2. Put into a 2-quart casserole. Dot with butter.
3. Bake, covered, at 350°F 1 hour, or until cabbage is tender.

6 servings

Scalloped Corn and Broccoli

¼ cup chopped onion
2 tablespoons butter or margarine
1 tablespoon flour
1¼ cups milk*
1 cup (4 ounces) shredded Cheddar cheese
1 can (12 ounces) whole kernel corn, drained
2 packages (10 ounces each) frozen broccoli spears, cooked and drained

1. Sauté onion in butter in a skillet. Stir in flour. Gradually add milk, stirring until thickened and smooth.
2. Add cheese, stirring until melted. Stir in corn.
3. Arrange broccoli in a 2-quart shallow baking dish.
4. Pour corn sauce over broccoli.
5. Bake, uncovered, at 350°F 30 minutes, or until heated through.

8 servings

* One-fourth cup of the drained corn liquid can be substituted for ¼ cup of the milk.

Brandied Carrots

4 cups thinly sliced carrots
¼ cup butter or margarine
¼ cup water
1 teaspoon lemon juice
½ teaspoon salt
¼ teaspoon pepper
¼ cup brandy
2 tablespoons snipped parsley

1. Put carrots into a large saucepan. Add butter and water. Cover and cook over moderate heat, stirring occasionally, until carrots are just crisp-tender (about 15 minutes).
2. Add lemon juice, salt, pepper, and brandy.
3. Put into a 1½-quart casserole. Cover and refrigerate overnight.
4. Bake, covered, at 350°F 30 minutes, or until heated through. Sprinkle with parsley.

8 servings

Deluxe Scalloped Potatoes

1 package (5.5 ounces) scalloped
   potatoes
2 tablespoons butter or margarine
2½ cups boiling water
⅔ cup milk
⅓ cup crumbled blue cheese

1. Empty potato slices into a 1½-quart casserole. Sprinkle with sauce mix.
2. Stir in butter, water, milk, and blue cheese.
3. Bake, uncovered, at 400°F 30 to 35 minutes, or until potatoes are tender. Let stand a few minutes before serving.

4 servings

Apple-Honey Sweet Potatoes

4 sweet potatoes
4 cooking apples
½ cup honey
¼ teaspoon nutmeg

1. Bake sweet potatoes at 350°F 45 minutes, or until tender.
2. Core apples and cut into thin slices. (To avoid darkening, brush with lemon juice.)
3. Peel baked potatoes and cut into ½-inch-thick slices.
4. Alternate layers of potatoes and apples in a greased 2½-quart casserole. Drizzle with honey and sprinkle with nutmeg.
5. Bake, covered, at 350°F 20 minutes, or until heated through.

6 servings

Pecan Sweet Potatoes

¼ cup butter or margarine
2 tablespoons cornstarch
¾ cup firmly packed brown sugar
½ teaspoon salt
2 cups orange juice
2 cans (23 ounces each) sweet
   potatoes, drained
¼ cup chopped pecans

1. Melt butter in a saucepan. Blend cornstarch, brown sugar, and salt; mix with butter. Gradually add orange juice, stirring until thickened and clear.
2. Put sweet potatoes into a 1½-quart casserole. Pour sauce over sweet potatoes. Sprinkle with pecans.
3. Bake, covered, at 350°F 45 minutes, or until heated through.

8 servings

Spinach Bake

2 packages (10 ounces each) frozen chopped spinach, thawed and drained
2 cups milk
6 eggs
½ teaspoon salt
1 tablespoon instant minced onion
¾ cup (3 ounces) shredded Swiss cheese

1. Blend spinach, milk, eggs, and salt in a blender.
2. Pour into an 8-inch square baking dish. Sprinkle with onion and cheese.
3. Bake, uncovered, at 325°F 45 minutes, or until set. Let stand a few minutes. Cut into squares to serve.

6 servings

Spinach-Artichoke Casserole

1 jar (6 ounces) marinated artichoke hearts, drained
2 packages (10 ounces each) frozen chopped spinach, cooked and squeezed
1 package (8 ounces) cream cheese, softened
2 tablespoons butter or margarine, softened
¼ cup milk
½ teaspoon freshly ground pepper
¼ cup (1 ounce) grated Parmesan cheese

1. Put artichoke hearts into a 1½-quart casserole.
2. Spread spinach over artichoke hearts.
3. Beat together cream cheese and butter. Gradually add milk, beating until smooth. Spread over spinach.
4. Sprinkle pepper and Parmesan cheese over top.
5. Bake, covered, at 350°F 30 minutes. Remove cover. Garnish with **pimento strips** and **hard-cooked egg slices.** Bake an additional 10 minutes, or until heated through.

6 servings

Spinach and Rice

1 package (10 ounces) frozen chopped spinach, cooked and drained
1 can (10¾ ounces) condensed cream of mushroom soup
1½ cups boiling water
1⅓ cups packaged precooked rice
⅛ teaspoon garlic powder
1 teaspoon lemon juice
2 hard-cooked eggs, sliced
¾ cup (3 ounces) shredded Cheddar cheese
1 can (3 ounces) French-fried onions

1. Combine spinach, soup, boiling water, rice, garlic powder, and lemon juice. Put into a 1½-quart shallow baking dish.
2. Bake, covered, at 400°F 25 minutes, or until rice is tender. Remove cover and stir. Arrange eggs over top. Sprinkle with cheese. Place onions around edge. Bake an additional 5 minutes, or until cheese is melted.

4 servings

Sweet and Sour Red Cabbage

1 head (2 pounds) red cabbage
4 tablespoons brown sugar
1 teaspoon salt
½ cup beef bouillon
¼ cup cider vinegar
4 slices bacon, diced
4 tablespoons butter
2 medium cooking (sour) apples, pared and sliced
1 cup red wine

1. Discard tough, outer leaves of cabbage and shred, as for cole slaw.
2. Combine brown sugar, salt, bouillon, and vinegar as a marinade. Let cabbage stand in marinade 1 hour or longer. (This cabbage is limp when served so can be marinated as long as you wish.)
3. Cook bacon until crisp; drain bacon pieces, and pour off all but 2 tablespoons of bacon fat.
4. Melt butter in bacon fat. Add cabbage, marinade and all. Arrange apples on top of cabbage. Cover and cook slowly 1 hour.
5. Add wine, cover, and simmer 30 minutes.

6 servings

Macaroni Vegetable Medley au Vin

2 cups (8 ounces) elbow macaroni
1 package (10 ounces) frozen mixed vegetables
2 tablespoons butter or margarine
3 ounces fresh mushrooms, chopped
½ cup chopped onion
1 can (about 10 ounces) condensed cream of celery soup
1 soup can milk
2 teaspoons Worcestershire sauce
1 teaspoon salt
¼ teaspoon white pepper
1 teaspoon dry mustard
½ cup dry sherry or dry white wine
¼ cup chopped pimento
1 cup cooked peas
½ pound Swiss cheese, shredded
Chopped parsley
Pimento strips

1. Cook macaroni and frozen vegetables following directions on package. Drain and set aside.
2. Heat butter in a skillet; add mushrooms and onion. Cook, stirring occasionally, until onion is soft; set aside.
3. In a large bowl mix soup, milk, Worcestershire sauce, salt, white pepper, dry mustard, and wine. Add chopped pimento, peas, cheese, mushroom mixture, mixed vegetables, and macaroni; mix well. Turn into a greased 2½-quart casserole.
4. Bake at 300°F until thoroughly heated, about 30 minutes. Garnish with chopped parsley and pimento strips.

About 8 servings

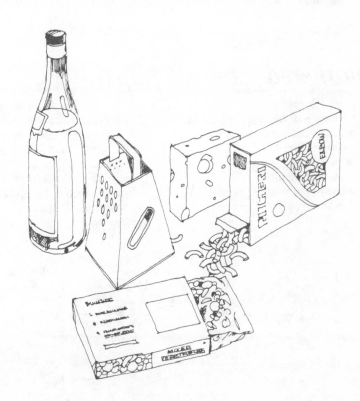

MEAT

Lamb Crown Roast with Mint Stuffing

8 slices enriched white bread,
    toasted and cubed
1 unpared red apple, cored and
    diced
1½ tablespoons coarsely chopped
    mint or 1½ teaspoons dried
    mint flakes
¾ teaspoon poultry seasoning
½ teaspoon salt
6 tablespoons butter
½ cup chopped celery
¼ cup chopped onion
½ cup water
1 lamb rib crown roast (5 to 6
    pounds)

1. Combine toasted bread cubes, apple, mint, poultry seasoning, and salt in a large bowl.
2. Heat butter in a saucepan. Mix in celery and onion and cook about 5 minutes. Pour over bread mixture along with water; toss lightly.
3. Place lamb on a rack, rib ends up, in a shallow roasting pan. Fill center with stuffing.
4. Roast in a 325°F oven about 2½ hours, or until a meat thermometer registers 175° to 180°F (depending on desired degree of doneness).
5. Place roast on a heated serving platter. Prepare gravy, if desired. Accompany with Parsley-Buttered New Potatoes and Butter-Sauced Asparagus.

About 8 servings

Smothered Lamb Chops

6 lamb rib chops
2 tablespoons butter or margarine
4 medium red potatoes, pared and
    thinly sliced
2 large onions, sliced
1½ cups beef bouillon
2 tablespoons snipped parsley
¼ cup buttered bread crumbs

1. Brown lamb chops on both sides in butter in a skillet. Place in a 2-quart shallow baking dish.
2. Arrange potatoes over chops and onions over potatoes. Season lightly with **salt.** Pour bouillon over all.
3. Bake, covered, at 375°F 1 hour, or until chops and vegetables are tender. Combine parsley and bread crumbs. Remove cover from casserole. Sprinkle with the parsley-bread crumbs. Bake, uncovered, at 450°F 10 minutes, or until crumbs are lightly browned.

6 servings

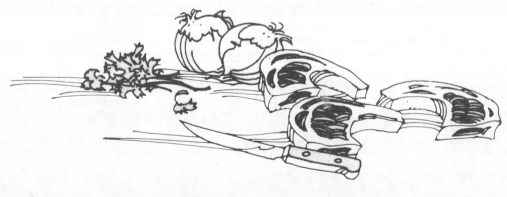

Roast Leg of Lamb with Spicy Wine Sauce

1 cup dry red wine
¼ cup salad oil
1 onion, coarsely chopped
2 cloves garlic, minced
½ teaspoon Tabasco
2 teaspoons salt
1 lamb leg whole (6 to 8 pounds)
  Parsley

1. Combine wine, oil, onion, garlic, Tabasco, and salt; pour over lamb. Cover and refrigerate 6 hours or overnight, turning occasionally.
2. Place lamb on rack in shallow roasting pan. Roast at 325°F about 25 minutes per pound, or until meat thermometer registers 160° to 170°F (medium); baste occasionally with marinade.
3. Garnish with parsley.

12 to 16 servings

Lamb Kabobs

1½ pounds lamb (leg, loin, or shoulder), boneless, cut in 1½-inch cubes
½ cup vegetable oil
1 tablespoon lemon juice
2 teaspoons sugar
½ teaspoon salt
½ teaspoon paprika
¼ teaspoon dry mustard
⅛ teaspoon ground black pepper
¼ teaspoon Worcestershire sauce
1 clove garlic, cut in halves
6 small whole cooked potatoes
6 small whole cooked onions
  Butter or margarine, melted
6 plum tomatoes

1. Put lamb cubes into a shallow dish. Combine oil, lemon juice, sugar, salt, paprika, dry mustard, pepper, Worcestershire sauce, and garlic. Pour over meat. Cover and marinate at least 1 hour in refrigerator, turning pieces occasionally. Drain.
2. Alternately thread lamb cubes, potatoes, and onions on 6 skewers. Brush pieces with melted butter.
3. Broil 3 to 4 inches from heat about 15 minutes, or until lamb is desired degree of doneness; turn frequently and brush with melted butter. Shortly before kabobs are done, impale tomatoes on ends of skewers.

6 servings

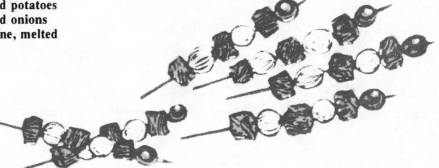

Lamb Curry

1½ pounds boneless lamb shoulder, cut in ¾-inch cubes
2 tablespoons shortening
1 teaspoon salt
1 teaspoon paprika
¼ teaspoon pepper
1 large onion, sliced
1 cup sliced celery
2¼ cups water
1 teaspoon curry powder
¼ cup flour
1 cup uncooked white rice

1. Brown lamb in shortening in a large saucepan. Sprinkle with salt, paprika, and pepper. Add onion, celery, and 2 cups water. Cover and simmer 1 hour, or until tender.
2. Combine curry powder, flour, and remaining ¼ cup water. Gradually add to saucepan, stirring until thickened and smooth.
3. Meanwhile, prepare rice according to package directions. Press rice in bottom and up sides of a 2-quart casserole. Pour lamb mixture into rice shell.
4. Bake, covered, at 350°F 20 minutes, or until casserole is bubbly. Serve with **chopped peanuts, shredded coconut, and chutney.**

6 servings

Chinatown Chop Suey

1¼ pounds pork, boneless
1 pound beef, boneless
¾ pound veal, boneless
3 tablespoons cooking oil
1 cup water
3 cups diagonally sliced celery
2 cups coarsely chopped onion
3 tablespoons cornstarch
¼ cup water
¼ cup soy sauce
¼ cup bead molasses
1 can (16 ounces) bean sprouts, drained and rinsed
2 cans (5 ounces each) water chestnuts, drained and sliced

1. Cut meat into 2x½x¼-inch strips. Heat oil in a large wok. Stir-fry ½ pound of meat at a time, browning pieces on all sides. Remove the meat from the wok as it is browned. When all the meat is browned, return it to the wok. Cover and cook over low heat 30 minutes.
2. Mix in 1 cup water, celery, and onions. Bring to boiling and simmer, covered, 20 minutes.
3. Blend cornstarch, the ¼ cup water, soy sauce, and molasses. Stir into meat mixture. Bring to boiling and cook 2 minutes, stirring constantly. Mix in bean sprouts and water chestnuts; heat.
4. Serve on **hot fluffy rice**.

8 servings

Savory Beef Stew

Beer adds a subtle flavor to the gravy, although it is not a typical beer taste. The alcohol boils off early in the cooking, so the dish may be served to children.

1½ pounds beef stew meat, boneless, cut in 1½-inch cubes
¼ cup flour
1 teaspoon salt
¼ teaspoon basil
¼ teaspoon savory or marjoram
⅛ teaspoon pepper
3 tablespoons vegetable oil
2 onions, sliced
1 can or bottle (12 ounces) beer
½ cup water
1 bay leaf
5 medium potatoes (1⅔ pounds)
1 pound carrots (8 to 10); or ½ pound each parsnips and carrots

1. Dredge meat in mixture of flour, salt, basil, savory, and pepper. Reserve excess flour. Brown meat in oil. Add onion, beer, water, and bay leaf. Cover and simmer 1½ hours.
2. Pare potatoes; cut into large cubes. Slice carrots and/or parsnips. Add vegetables to stew. If necessary, add a little more water.
3. Cover and simmer 1 hour more, or until meat and vegetables are tender. Make smooth paste of reserved flour mixture and a little water. Stir into stew during last 10 minutes of cooking.

6 servings

Lasagne Bolognese

3 tablespoons butter or margarine
3 tablespoons flour
1 cup milk
1 cup whipping cream
¼ teaspoon salt
Dash of pepper
½ pound lasagne noodles
Meat Sauce Bolognese
1 cup (4 ounces) grated Parmesan
cheese

1. Melt butter in a saucepan; blend in flour. Gradually add milk and cream, stirring until thickened and smooth. Add salt and pepper.
2. Cook lasagne noodles in **boiling salted water** according to package directions. Drain, rinse, and spread on a damp towel.
3. Spread a thin layer of Meat Sauce Bolognese in a 13x9-inch baking dish. Top with a layer of half the lasagne noodles, half the Meat Sauce Bolognese, half the white sauce, and half the cheese; repeat layers.
4. Bake, uncovered, at 375°F 35 to 40 minutes, or until mixture is bubbly and top is golden brown. Let stand 10 minutes. Cut into squares to serve.

8 servings

Meat Sauce Bolognese

6 bacon slices, diced
1 medium onion, chopped
½ cup chopped celery
½ cup chopped carrot
6 tablespoons butter or margarine
¼ pound chicken livers, diced
1 pound ground beef round
1 teaspoon salt
½ teaspoon oregano
¼ teaspoon nutmeg
1 bay leaf
2 tablespoons vinegar
1 can (8 ounces) tomato sauce
1 cup beef bouillon
1 cup sliced fresh mushrooms
½ cup dry white wine

1. Sauté bacon in a skillet; drain off all but 2 tablespoons fat. Add onion, celery, and carrot; cook until tender.
2. Add 2 tablespoons butter and the chicken livers. Brown lightly; add ground beef round. Cook 10 to 15 minutes, or until well browned.
3. Stir in salt, oregano, nutmeg, bay leaf, vinegar, tomato sauce, and bouillon. Cover and simmer ½ hour.
4. Sauté mushrooms in remaining 4 tablespoons butter. Add to meat sauce along with wine. Remove bay leaf. Simmer ½ hour longer.

1 quart

Beef and Pea Casserole

1 pound ground beef
1 medium onion, chopped
1 can (10¾ ounces) condensed
tomato soup
⅓ cup water
2 cups cooked noodles
1 can (8 ounces) peas, drained*
1 can (4 ounces) sliced mushrooms,
drained*

1. Brown ground beef and onion in a skillet; drain off excess fat. Combine with remaining ingredients. Put into a 2-quart casserole.
2. Bake, covered, at 350°F 30 minutes, or until heated through. To serve, sprinkle with **Parmesan cheese** and garnish with **pimento strips.**

6 servings

* The liquid from the peas or mushrooms may be substituted for the 1/3 cup water.

Oven Beef Bake

2 pounds beef stew meat, cut in
   1-inch cubes
1 can (10¾ ounces) condensed cream
   of mushroom soup
1 can (10½ ounces) condensed onion
   soup
¼ cup dry vermouth

1. Put meat into a 2-quart casserole.
2. Combine mushroom soup, onion soup, and vermouth. Pour over meat.
3. Bake, covered, at 325°F 3 hours, or until meat is tender. Serve with **hot, cooked noodles.**

8 servings

Swiss Steak Mozzarella

2 pounds beef round steak, ½ inch
   thick
3 tablespoons flour
½ cup butter or margarine
1 can (16 ounces) tomatoes, cut up
1¼ teaspoons salt
¼ teaspoon basil
½ cup chopped green pepper
1½ cups (6 ounces) mozzarella cheese

1. Cut meat into serving-size pieces; coat with flour.
2. Melt butter in a skillet. Brown meat slowly on both sides. Put into a 12x8-inch baking dish.
3. Combine tomatoes, salt, basil, and green pepper. Pour over meat.
4. Bake, covered, at 350°F 1 hour, or until meat is tender. Remove cover. Sprinkle with cheese and bake an additional 5 minutes, or until cheese is melted.

8 servings

Beef Bourguignon

¼ cup flour
1 teaspoon salt
½ teaspoon freshly ground black
   pepper
2 pounds beef stew meat, cut in
   2-inch cubes
¼ cup butter or margarine
1 medium onion, chopped
2 medium carrots, chopped
1 garlic clove, minced
2 cups dry red wine
1 can (6 ounces) mushroom crowns,
   drained, reserving liquid
1 bay leaf
3 tablespoons snipped parsley
½ teaspoon thyme
1 can (16 ounces) onions, drained

1. Combine flour, salt, and pepper; coat beef cubes.
2. Brown beef in butter in a skillet. Put into a 2-quart casserole.
3. Add onion, carrots, and garlic to skillet. Cook until tender but not brown. Add wine, liquid from mushrooms, bay leaf, parsley, and thyme. Pour over meat.
4. Bake, covered, at 350°F 2½ hours. Remove cover. Add onions and mushroom crowns. Bake an additional 30 minutes, or until meat is tender.

8 servings

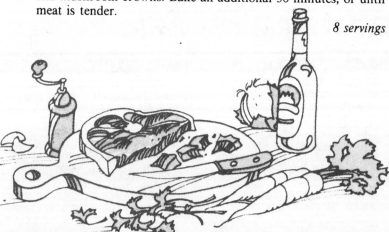

Pot Roast of Beef with Wine

3- to 4-pound beef pot roast, boneless (rump, chuck, or round)
2 cups red wine
2 medium onions, chopped
3 medium carrots, washed, pared,
  and sliced
1 clove garlic
1 bay leaf
¼ teaspoon pepper
4 sprigs parsley
¼ cup all-purpose flour
2 teaspoons salt
¼ teaspoon pepper
3 tablespoons butter
2 cups red wine
1 cup cold water
¼ cup all-purpose flour

1. Put the meat into a deep bowl. Add wine, onions, carrots, garlic, bay leaf, pepper, and parsley. Cover and put into refrigerator to marinate 12 hours, or overnight; turn meat occasionally. Drain the meat, reserving marinade, and pat meat dry with absorbent paper.
2. Coat meat evenly with a mixture of flour, salt, and pepper.
3. Heat butter in a large saucepot; brown the meat slowly on all sides in the butter. Drain off the fat. Add the marinade and wine. Cover and bring to boiling. Reduce heat and simmer slowly 2½ to 3 hours, or until meat is tender.
4. Remove meat to a warm platter.
5. Strain the cooking liquid. Return the strained liquid to saucepot.
6. Pour water into a screw-top jar and add flour; cover jar tightly and shake until mixture is well blended.
7. Stirring constantly, slowly pour one half of the blended mixture into liquid in saucepot. Bring to boiling. Gradually add only what is needed of the remaining blended mixture for consistency desired. Bring gravy to boiling after each addition. Cook 3 to 5 minutes longer.
8. Serve meat with gravy.

8 to 10 servings

Beef Burgundy

This is a family-size recipe. Increase it for a party, as pictured on the cover.

2 slices bacon
2 pounds beef round tip steak, cut
  in 2-inch cubes
2 tablespoons flour
1 teaspoon seasoned salt
1 package beef stew seasoning
  mix
1 cup burgundy
1 cup water
1 tablespoon tomato paste
12 small boiling onions
4 ounces fresh mushrooms, sliced
  and lightly browned in 1
  tablespoon butter or
  margarine
16 cherry tomatoes, stems
  removed

1. Fry bacon in a Dutch oven; remove bacon. Coat meat cubes with a blend of flour and seasoned salt. Add to fat in Dutch oven and brown thoroughly. Add beef stew seasoning mix, burgundy, water, and tomato paste. Cover and simmer gently 45 minutes.
2. Peel onions and pierce each end with a fork so they will retain their shape when cooked. Add onions to beef mixture and simmer 40 minutes, or until meat and onions are tender. Add mushrooms and cherry tomatoes; simmer 3 minutes. Pour into a serving dish.

6 to 8 servings

Note: If cherry tomatoes are not available, use canned whole peeled tomatoes.

Easy Corned Beef Bake

½ package (6 ounces) noodles, cooked
  and drained
1 can (12 ounces) corned beef, cut up
1 cup (4 ounces) shredded American
  cheese
¾ cup milk
¼ cup chopped onion
½ cup fine dry bread crumbs
2 tablespoons butter or margarine

1. Combine noodles, corned beef, cheese, milk, and onion. Put into a greased 1½-quart casserole.
2. Top with bread crumbs. Dot with butter.
3. Bake, covered, at 325°F 45 minutes, or until casserole is bubbly.

4 servings

Stuffed Veal Steak

· 4 veal loin top loin chops, 1 inch
thick (about 1½ pounds)
1 cup dry white wine, such as chablis
½ cup sliced mushrooms
1 green pepper, cut in ½-inch pieces
½ cup butter or margarine
½ cup all-purpose flour
1 egg, fork beaten
½ cup fine dry bread crumbs
½ cup grated Parmesan cheese
4 slices proscuitto (Italian ham)
4 slices (4 ounces) Cheddar cheese

1. Make a cut in the side of each veal chop, cutting almost all the way through. Lay each open and pound flat. Marinate meat for 1 hour in wine.

2. While meat marinates, sauté mushrooms and green pepper in butter for about 10 minutes or until tender. Remove from skillet with slotted spoon, leaving butter in skillet. Set vegetables aside.

3. Dry veal on paper towel. Bread on one side only, dipping first in flour, then in beaten egg, and last in bread crumbs mixed with Parmesan cheese.

4. Lay a slice of proscuitto on one half of unbreaded side of veal. Fold other side over. Panfry for 6 minutes on one side in butter in skillet, adding more butter if needed. Turn veal, and remove skillet from heat.

5. Insert a slice of cheese and ¼ of the mushroom-pepper mixture into the fold of each steak.

6. Return to heat and cook 6 minutes, or until meat is tender.

4 servings

Veal Cutlet in Wine with Olives

1½ pounds veal cutlets, cut about ¼
inch thick
¼ cup all-purpose flour
1 teaspoon salt
½ teaspoon monosodium
glutamate
¼ teaspoon pepper
2 to 3 tablespoons butter or
margarine
⅓ cup marsala
⅓ cup sliced green olives

1. Place meat on flat working surface and pound with meat hammer to increase tenderness. Turn meat and repeat process. Cut into 6 serving-size pieces. Coat with a mixture of flour, salt, monosodium glutamate, and pepper.

2. Heat butter in skillet over low heat. Brown meat over medium heat. Add marsala and green olives. Cover skillet and cook over low heat about 1 hour, or until meat is tender when pierced with a fork.

About 6 servings

Veal Glacé

1 cup dry white wine
1½ teaspoons tarragon leaves
1½ pounds veal cutlets (about ¼ inch thick)
3 tablespoons butter
½ teaspoon salt
⅛ teaspoon ground black pepper
½ cup condensed consommé (undiluted)
½ cup dry vermouth

1. Stir tarragon into white wine. Cover; allow to stand several hours, stirring occasionally.
2. Cut meat into pieces about 3×2 inches. Heat butter in skillet until lightly browned. Add meat and brown lightly. Season with salt and pepper. Reduce heat and pour in tarragon wine mixture with the consommé and vermouth. Simmer uncovered, about 10 minutes, or until veal is tender.
3. Remove veal to a heated dish and cover. Increase heat under skillet and cook sauce until it is reduced to a thin glaze (about 10 minutes), stirring occasionally.
4. Pour glaze over meat, turning meat to coat evenly. Serve hot.

About 6 servings

Note: If desired, accompany with buttered fluffy rice tossed with chopped parsley and toasted slivered almonds.

Curried Veal and Vegetables

1 pound veal for stew (1-inch cubes)
2 cups water
1 teaspoon salt
3 medium carrots, pared and cut in quarters
½ pound green beans
2 large stalks celery, cut in ½-inch slices
3 tablespoons butter or margarine
2 tablespoons flour
½ teaspoon curry powder
¼ teaspoon salt
Cooked rice
Fresh parsley, snipped

1. Put veal into a large saucepan with water and 1 teaspoon salt. Cover, bring to boiling, reduce heat, and simmer 1 hour. Add carrots, green beans, and celery. Cover, bring to boiling, and simmer 1 hour, or until meat is tender.
2. Remove meat and vegetables from broth with a slotted spoon; set aside. Reserve broth.
3. Heat butter in a saucepan. Blend in flour, curry powder, and ¼ teaspoon salt. Heat until bubbly. Add reserved broth gradually, stirring until smooth. Bring to boiling, stirring constantly, and cook 1 to 2 minutes. Mix in meat and vegetables. Heat thoroughly.
4. Serve over rice. Sprinkle with parsley.

About 6 servings

German Veal Chops

4 veal loin or rib chops
Butter or margarine
2 medium onions, sliced
1 cup dark beer
1 bay leaf
½ teaspoon salt
Dash pepper
2 tablespoons flour

1. Brown veal in butter in a skillet; set meat aside. Sauté onion in same skillet until golden.
2. Add beer, bay leaf, salt, and pepper. Cover and simmer 15 minutes.
3. Transfer veal and onion to a platter. Make a paste of flour and a little water; stir into cooking liquid in skillet. Cook, stirring constantly, until thickened and smooth. Pour over veal and onion.

4 servings

Note: If you do not have dark beer, add ½ **teaspoon molasses** to light beer.

Pork Loin Roast

1 pork loin roast (4 to 6 pounds)
Salt and pepper
Spiced crab apples

1. Have the meat retailer saw across the rib bones of roast at base of the backbone, separating the ribs from the backbone. Place roast, fat side up, on a rack in an open roasting pan. Season with salt and pepper. Insert meat thermometer in roast so the bulb is centered in the thickest part and not resting on bone or in fat.
2. Roast in a 350°F oven about 2½ to 3 hours, or until thermometer registers 170°F; allow 30 to 40 minutes per pound.
3. For easy carving, remove backbone, place roast on platter, and allow roast to set for 15 to 20 minutes. Garnish platter with spiced crab apples, heated if desired. Accompany with Hash Brown Potatoes au Gratin.

8 to 10 servings

Breaded Pork Chops with Beer Gravy

4 pork chops, cut ½ to ¾ inch thick
1 egg
1 tablespoon water
½ cup fine cracker crumbs (from about 12 saltines)
½ teaspoon salt
¼ teaspoon paprika
2 tablespoons oil
¾ cup beer
2 tablespoons flour
¾ cup beef bouillon
1 tablespoon ketchup

1. Dip chops in a mixture of egg and water, coating both sides. Mix crumbs, salt, and paprika. Dip egg-coated chops in this mixture, coating both sides well.
2. Brown chops slowly in oil, cooking about 15 minutes. Reduce heat; add ¼ cup beer. Cover and simmer 20 to 30 minutes, or until done.
3. Make a paste of flour and a little remaining beer. Place chops on platter. Stir flour paste, rest of beer, bouillon, and ketchup into cooking liquid. Cook, stirring constantly, until thickened. Season to taste, if desired. (Makes enough gravy to pour over meat and potatoes.)

4 servings

Bavarian Casserole

A good use for leftover roast pork.

2 celery stalks, chopped
1 medium onion, chopped
3 tablespoons butter or margarine
½ teaspoon salt
¼ teaspoon sage
¼ teaspoon sugar
⅛ teaspoon pepper
1 cup beer
4 cups pumpernickel bread cubes (5 slices)
2 cups cubed cooked pork (10 ounces)

1. Sauté celery and onion in butter until soft; stir in seasonings. Add beer.
2. Place bread and pork in a 1½-quart casserole. Add beer-vegetable mixture. Stir lightly.
3. Cover and bake at 375°F 30 to 35 minutes.

4 servings

Lagered Ham and Noodle Casserole

Beer delicately flavors the cheese sauce in this delicious family-style casserole.

1 **medium green pepper, chopped**
1 **medium onion, chopped**
¼ **cup butter or margarine**
3 **tablespoons flour**
½ **teaspoon dry mustard**
½ **teaspoon salt**
  Dash pepper
⅓ **cup instant nonfat dry milk**
1 **can or bottle (12 ounces) beer**
1 **cup shredded Cheddar cheese**
  (4 ounces)
8 **ounces uncooked medium**
  noodles, cooked and drained
2 **cups diced cooked ham (⅔**
  pound)

1. For sauce, slowly sauté green peeper and onion in butter until soft and almost tender. Stir in flour and seasonings.
2. Mix dry milk and ⅓ cup beer.
3. Gradually add remaining beer to flour mixture. Cook, stirring constantly, until thickened and bubbly. Add cheese; stir until melted. Remove from heat; add beer-milk mixture.
4. Combine sauce, cooked noodles, and ham. Turn into a 2½-quart casserole.
5. Bake at 350°F 20 minutes, or until heated through and bubbly.

6 servings

Fruited Pork Roast, Scandinavian Style

Prunes and apple are stuffed inside a boneless pork roast to create an unusual entrée that's nice for a party or a special family meal. The slices are especially attractive. The sweetened sauce retains just a hint of beer flavor.

1 **pork rolled loin roast, boneless,**
  (3 to 3½ pounds)
8 to 10 **pitted dried prunes**
1 **can or bottle (12 ounces) beer**
½ **teaspoon ginger**
1 **medium apple, pared and**
  chopped
1 **teaspoon lemon juice**
½ **teaspoon salt**
  Dash pepper
¼ **cup flour**

1. Make pocket down center of roast by piercing with a long, sharp tool such as a steel knife sharpener; leave strings on roast. (Alternate method: Remove strings. Using strong knife, cut pocket in pork by making a deep slit down length of loin, going to within ½ inch of the two ends and within 1 inch of other side.)
2. Meanwhile, combine prunes, beer, and ginger in a saucepan; heat to boiling. Remove from heat; let stand 30 minutes.
3. Mix apple with lemon juice to prevent darkening. Drain prunes, reserving liquid; pat dry with paper towels. Mix prunes and apple.
4. Pack fruit into pocket in pork, using handle of wooden spoon to pack tightly. (With alternate method of cutting pocket, tie with string at 1-inch intervals. Secure with skewers or sew with kitchen thread.)
5. Place meat on rack in a roasting pan.
6. Roast at 350°F 2 to 2½ hours, allowing 40 to 45 minutes per pound. During last 45 minutes of roasting, spoon fat from pan; baste occasionally with liquid drained from prunes.
7. Transfer meat to a platter. Skim fat from cooking liquid; measure liquid. Add a little water to roasting pan to help loosen brown bits; add to cooking liquid. Add salt, pepper, and enough additional water to measure 2 cups total. Make a paste of flour and a little more water. Combine with cooking liquid. Cook, stirring constantly, until thickened. Pass in a sauceboat for pouring over meat slices.

8 servings

Northwoods Pork Chops

1 package (2¾ ounces) instant wild rice
¼ cup chopped celery
¼ cup chopped green pepper
¼ cup chopped onion
6 tablespoons butter or margarine
4 pork chops, ¾ inch thick
¼ cup flour
2 cups milk
½ teaspoon salt
⅛ teaspoon pepper
½ cup (2 ounces) shredded American cheese

1. Prepare wild rice according to package directions.
2. Sauté celery, green pepper, and onion in 4 tablespoons butter in a skillet. Combine with wild rice. Put into a 1½-quart shallow baking dish.
3. Brown pork chops on both sides in skillet. Place on top of wild rice mixture.
4. Melt remaining 2 tablespoons butter in skillet. Blend in flour. Gradually add milk, stirring until thickened and smooth. Add salt and pepper. Pour over pork chops.
5. Bake, covered, at 350°F 1 hour, or until chops are done. Sprinkle with cheese.

4 servings

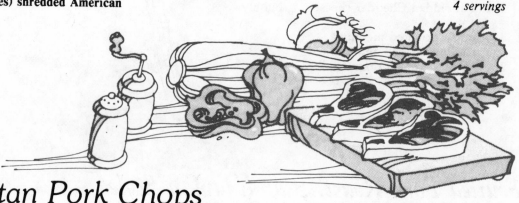

Neapolitan Pork Chops

2 tablespoons olive oil
1 clove garlic, minced
6 pork loin rib chops, cut about ¾ to 1 inch thick
1 teaspoon salt
½ teaspoon monosodium glutamate
¼ teaspoon pepper
1 pound mushrooms
2 green peppers
½ cup canned tomatoes, sieved
3 tablespoons dry white wine

1. Heat oil in large heavy skillet, add minced garlic and cook until lightly browned.
2. Season pork chops with a mixture of the salt, monosodium glutamate, and pepper. Place in skillet and slowly brown chops on both sides.
3. While chops brown, clean and slice mushrooms and chop green peppers; set aside.
4. When chops are browned, add the mushrooms and peppers. Stir in tomatoes and wine, cover skillet and cook over low heat 1 to 1½ hours, depending on thickness of chops. Add small amounts of water as needed. Test the chops for tenderness by piercing with a fork.

6 servings

Apple-Covered Ham in Claret

2 smoked ham center slices, fully cooked, about ¾ inch thick (about ½ pound each) or 1 large center cut 1½ inches thick
½ teaspoon dry mustard
3 to 4 medium Golden Delicious apples, cored and cut in rings
4 orange slices
¾ cup dry red wine, such as claret
½ cup packed brown sugar
Parsley sprigs

1. Place ham slices in large shallow baking dish. Sprinkle each slice with ¼ teaspoon mustard.
2. Cut unpared apple rings in half and place around outer edge of ham, slightly overlapping slices.
3. Place two orange slices in center of each ham slice.
4. Pour wine over top of ham and fruit. Then sprinkle entire dish with brown sugar.
5. Cover; cook in a 350°F oven 45 minutes. Serve on platter or from baking dish, and garnish with parsley.

6 to 8 servings

Super Sausage Supper

1 cup chopped onion
1 garlic clove, minced
3 carrots, pared and thinly sliced
2 tablespoons shortening
1 jar (32 ounces) sauerkraut, drained
2 cups apple cider
½ cup dry white wine
¼ teaspoon pepper
3 parsley sprigs
1 bay leaf
1 package (12 ounces) pork sausage
    links, cooked and drained
1 package (5 ounces) tiny smoked
    sausage links
2 links (8 ounces each) Polish
    sausage, cooked and drained
2 cans (16 ounces each) small white
    potatoes, drained
1 apple, cored and cut in chunks

1. Sauté onion, garlic, and carrot in shortening in a skillet. Add sauerkraut, apple cider, wine, pepper, parsley, and bay leaf. Bring to a boil; reduce heat and simmer 15 minutes.
2. Stir in remaining ingredients. Remove bay leaf. Put into a 3-quart casserole.
3. Bake, covered, at 350°F 1 hour.

8 servings

Hearty Sausage Supper

1 jar (16 ounces) applesauce
1 can (14 ounces) sauerkraut, drained
⅓ cup dry white wine
2 tablespoons firmly packed brown
    sugar
1 can (16 ounces) small white
    potatoes, drained
1 can (16 ounces) small whole onions,
    drained
1 ring (12 ounces) Polish sausage,
    slashed several times
1 tablespoon snipped parsley

1. Mix applesauce, sauerkraut, wine, and brown sugar. Put into a 2½-quart casserole.
2. Arrange potatoes and onions around edge of casserole. Place sausage in center.
3. Bake, covered, at 350°F 45 to 50 minutes, or until heated through. Sprinkle with parsley.

4 servings

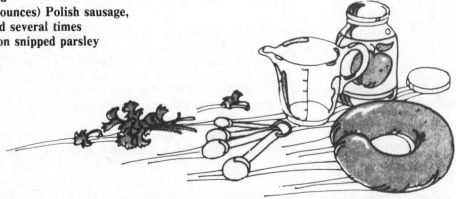

POULTRY

Chicken and Dumplings

¼ cup butter or margarine
2 broiler-fryer chickens, cut in serving-size pieces
½ cup chopped onion
¼ cup chopped celery
2 tablespoons chopped celery leaves
1 clove garlic, minced
¼ cup enriched all-purpose flour
4 cups chicken broth
1 teaspoon sugar
2 teaspoons salt
¼ teaspoon ground black pepper
1 teaspoon basil leaves
2 bay leaves
¼ cup chopped parsley
Basil Dumplings
2 packages (10 ounces each) frozen green peas

1. Heat butter in a large skillet. Add chicken pieces and brown on all sides. Remove chicken from skillet.
2. Add onion, celery, celery leaves, and garlic to fat in skillet. Cook until vegetables are tender. Sprinkle with flour and mix well. Add chicken broth, sugar, salt, pepper, basil, bay leaves, and parsley; bring to boiling, stirring constantly. Return chicken to skillet and spoon sauce over it; cover.
3. Cook in a 350°F oven 40 minutes.
4. Shortly before cooking time is completed, prepare Basil Dumplings.
5. Remove skillet from oven and turn control to 425°F. Stir peas into skillet mixture and bring to boiling. Drop dumpling dough onto stew.
6. Return to oven and cook, uncovered, 10 minutes; cover and cook 10 minutes, or until chicken is tender and dumplings are done.

About 8 servings

Basil Dumplings: Combine **2 cups all-purpose biscuit mix** and **1 teaspoon basil leaves** in a bowl. Add **⅔ cup milk** and stir with a fork until a dough is formed. Proceed as directed in recipe.

Chicken Fricassee with Vegetables

1 broiler-fryer chicken (about 3 pounds), cut in serving-size pieces
1½ teaspoons salt
1 bay leaf
Water
2 cups sliced carrots
2 onions, quartered
2 crookneck squashes, cut in halves lengthwise
2 pattypan squashes, cut in halves
Green beans (about 6 ounces), tips cut off
1 can (3½ ounces) pitted ripe olives, drained
1 tablespoon cornstarch
2 tablespoons water

1. Place chicken pieces along with salt and bay leaf in a Dutch oven or saucepot. Add enough water to just cover chicken. Bring to boiling; simmer, covered, 25 minutes until chicken is almost tender.
2. Add carrots and onions to cooking liquid; cook, covered, 10 minutes. Add squashes and green beans to cooking liquid; cook, covered, 10 minutes, or until chicken and vegetables are tender. Remove chicken and vegetables to a warm serving dish and add olives; keep hot.
3. Blend cornstarch and 2 tablespoons water; stir into boiling cooking liquid. Boil 2 to 3 minutes. Pour gravy over chicken.

About 4 servings

Chicken Polynesian Style

2 cups chicken broth
1 package (10 ounces) frozen mixed
　　vegetables
½ cup diagonally sliced celery
1½ tablespoons cornstarch
1 teaspoon monosodium glutamate
½ teaspoon sugar
½ teaspoon seasoned salt
⅛ teaspoon ground black pepper
½ teaspoon Worcestershire sauce
1 small clove garlic, minced or
　　crushed in a garlic press
1 tablespoon instant minced onion
1 can (6 ounces) ripe olives, drained
　　and cut in wedges
　　Cooked chicken, cut in 1-inch
　　pieces (about 2 cups)
　　Chow mein noodles
　　Salted peanuts
　　Soy sauce

1. Heat ½ cup chicken broth in a saucepan. Add frozen vegetables and celery; cook, covered, until crisp-tender. Remove vegetables and set aside; reserve any cooking liquid in saucepan.
2. Mix cornstarch, monosodium glutamate, sugar, seasoned salt, and pepper; blend with ¼ cup of the chicken broth. Add remaining broth, Worcestershire sauce, garlic, and onion to the saucepan. Add cornstarch mixture; bring to boiling, stirring constantly. Cook and stir 2 to 3 minutes.
3. Mix in olives, chicken, and reserved vegetables; heat thoroughly, stirring occasionally.
4. Serve over chow mein noodles and top generously with peanuts. Accompany with a cruet of soy sauce.

About 6 servings

Country Captain

1 broiler-fryer chicken (3 to 3½
　　pounds), cut in serving-size
　　pieces
¼ cup enriched all-purpose flour
½ teaspoon salt
　　Pinch ground white pepper
3 to 4 tablespoons lard
2 onions, finely chopped
2 medium green peppers, chopped
1 clove garlic, crushed in a garlic
　　press or minced
1½ teaspoons salt
½ teaspoon ground white pepper
1½ teaspoons curry powder
½ teaspoon ground thyme
½ teaspoon snipped parsley
5 cups undrained canned tomatoes
2 cups hot cooked rice
¼ cup dried currants
¾ cup roasted blanched almonds
　　Parsley sprigs

1. Remove skin from chicken. Mix flour, ½ teaspoon salt, and pinch white pepper. Coat chicken pieces.
2. Melt lard in a large heavy skillet; add chicken and brown on all sides. Remove pieces from skillet and keep hot.
3. Cook onions, peppers, and garlic in the same skillet, stirring occasionally until onion is lightly browned. Blend 1½ teaspoons salt, ½ teaspoon white pepper, curry powder, and thyme. Mix into skillet along with parsley and tomatoes.
4. Arrange chicken in a shallow roasting pan and pour tomato mixture over it. (If it does not cover chicken, add a small amount of water to the skillet in which mixture was cooked and pour liquid over chicken.) Place a cover on pan or cover tightly with aluminum foil.
5. Cook in a 350°F oven about 45 minutes, or until chicken is tender.
6. Arrange chicken in center of a large heated platter and pile the hot rice around it. Stir currants into sauce remaining in the pan and pour over the rice. Scatter almonds over top. Garnish with parsley.

About 6 servings

Chicken with Fruit

1 tablespoon flour
1 teaspoon seasoned salt
¾ teaspoon paprika
3 pounds broiler-fryer chicken
    pieces (legs, thighs, and breasts)
1½ tablespoons vegetable oil
1½ tablespoons butter or margarine
1 glove garlic, crushed in a garlic
    press or minced
⅓ cup chicken broth
2 tablespoons cider vinegar
1 tablespoon brown sugar
¼ teaspoon rosemary
1 can (11 ounces) mandarin
    oranges, drained; reserve syrup
1 jar (4 ounces) maraschino
    cherries, drained; reserve syrup
1 tablespoon water
1 tablespoon cornstarch
½ cup dark seedless raisins
    Cooked rice

1. Mix flour, seasoned salt, and paprika. Coat chicken pieces.
2. Heat oil, butter, and garlic in a large heavy skillet. Add chicken pieces and brown well on all sides.
3. Mix broth, vinegar, brown sugar, rosemary, and reserved syrups. Pour into skillet; cover and cook slowly 25 minutes, or until chicken is tender.
4. Remove chicken pieces to a serving dish and keep warm; skim any excess fat from liquid in skillet. Blend water with cornstarch and stir into liquid in skillet. Add raisins, bring to boiling, stirring constantly, and cook about 5 minutes, or until mixture is thickened and smooth. Mix in orange sections and cherries; heat thoroughly.
5. Pour sauce over chicken and serve with hot fluffy rice.

About 6 servings

Chicken Livers and Mushrooms

2 pounds chicken livers, thawed if
    frozen
½ cup enriched all-purpose flour
1 teaspoon salt
¼ teaspoon ground white pepper
⅓ cup butter or margarine
1 cup orange sections, cut in halves
1 can (6 ounces) broiled mushrooms
    Fresh parsley, snipped

1. Rinse chicken livers and drain on absorbent paper. Mix flour, salt, and pepper; coat chicken livers evenly.
2. Heat butter in a large skillet, add chicken livers, and cook 10 minutes, or until livers are lightly browned and tender. Mix in orange sections; heat.
3. Meanwhile, heat mushrooms in their broth in a small skillet.
4. Arrange cooked chicken livers and heated orange sections on a hot platter. Top with mushrooms and sprinkle with parsley. Serve immediately.

About 6 servings

Chicken Mexicana

3 tablespoons vegetable oil
2 broiler-fryer chickens (2½ to 3
    pounds each), cut in serving-size
    pieces
2 cans (8 ounces each) tomato sauce
1 can (13¾ ounces) chicken broth
2 tablespoons (½ envelope) dry onion
    soup mix
¾ cup chopped onion
1 clove garlic, minced
6 tablespoons crunchy peanut butter
½ cup cream
½ teaspoon chili powder
¼ cup dry sherry
    Cooked rice

1. Heat oil in a large skillet. Add chicken and brown on all sides.
2. Meanwhile, combine tomato sauce, 1 cup chicken broth, soup mix, onion, and garlic in a saucepan. Heat thoroughly, stirring constantly.
3. Pour sauce over chicken in skillet. Simmer, covered, 20 minutes.
4. Put peanut butter into a bowl and blend in cream and remaining chicken broth; stir into skillet along with chili powder and sherry. Heat thoroughly. Serve with hot fluffy rice.

About 6 servings

Crunchy Fried Chicken

Chicken is dipped in a beer batter, then fried. The resulting coating is tender, crisp, and so delicious!

1 cup all-purpose flour
½ teaspoon salt
¼ teaspoon pepper
2 eggs
½ cup beer
1 broiler-fryer chicken (2 to 2½ pounds), cut up
Cooking oil

1. Mix flour, salt, and pepper. Beat eggs with beer; add to flour mixture. Stir until smooth.
2. Dip chicken in batter, coating pieces well. Chill 1 hour.
3. Fry chicken in hot oil ½ to 1 inch deep 15 minutes on one side. Turn; fry on other side 5 to 10 minutes, or until browned and done. Drain on absorbent paper.

4 servings

Chicken Easy Oriental Style

¼ cup flour
1 teaspoon salt
¼ teaspoon pepper
4 chicken breasts, split in halves
¼ cup shortening
1 can (10¾ ounces) condensed cream of chicken soup
¼ cup dry white wine
¼ cup milk
1 can (4 ounces) water chestnuts, drained and sliced
¼ teaspoon ground ginger

1. Combine flour, salt, and pepper; coat chicken with mixture.
2. Brown chicken in shortening in skillet. Place in a 13x9-inch baking dish.
3. Combine soup, wine, milk, chestnuts, and ginger. Pour over chicken.
4. Bake, covered, at 350°F 1 hour, or until chicken is tender. If desired, sprinkle with snipped parsley.

4 servings

Chicken and Tomato Casserole

1 broiler-fryer chicken (about 3 pounds), cut up
3 tablespoons shortening
½ cup chopped onion
¼ cup chopped green pepper
1 can (28 ounces) tomatoes (undrained)
1 can (8 ounces) tomato sauce
1 can (6 ounces) tomato paste
1 teaspoon salt
1 teaspoon oregano

1. Brown chicken in shortening in a skillet. Place in a 2-quart casserole.
2. Sauté onion and green pepper in fat in skillet. Stir in remaining ingredients and pour over chicken.
3. Bake, covered, at 350°F 1 hour, or until chicken is tender. Serve with **hot, cooked spaghetti.**

4 servings

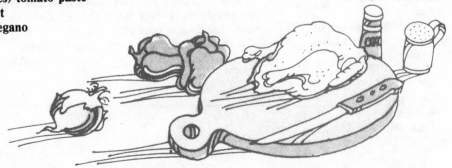

Chicken, Cacciatore Style

¼ cup vegetable oil
1 broiler-fryer chicken (about 2½ pounds), cut in serving-size pieces
2 medium onions, sliced
2 cloves garlic, crushed in a garlic press or minced
3 tomatoes, sliced
2 medium green peppers, sliced
1 small bay leaf
1 teaspoon salt
¼ teaspoon ground black pepper
½ teaspoon celery seed
1 teaspoon crushed oregano or basil
1 can (8 ounces) tomato sauce
¼ cup dry white wine
8 ounces spaghetti, cooked

1. Heat oil in a large heavy skillet. Add chicken and brown on all sides. Remove chicken from skillet.
2. Add onion and garlic to oil remaining in skillet and cook until onion is tender but not brown; stir occasionally to cook evenly.
3. Return chicken to skillet and add the tomato, green pepper, and bay leaf.
4. Mix salt, pepper, celery seed, and oregano with tomato sauce; pour over all.
5. Cover and cook over low heat 45 minutes. Blend in wine and cook, uncovered, 20 minutes. Discard bay leaf.
6. Put cooked spaghetti onto a warm serving platter and top with the chicken pieces and sauce.

About 6 servings

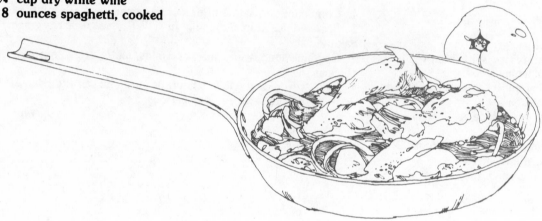

Herb-Chicken with Mushrooms

2 tablespoons butter or margarine
1 broiler-fryer chicken (3 pounds), cut in quarters
¾ cup cider vinegar
¼ cup water
1 cup (about 3 ounces) sliced mushrooms
1 tablespoon finely chopped parsley
1 tablespoon finely chopped chives
1 teaspoon crushed tarragon
½ teaspoon thyme
½ teaspoon salt
¼ teaspoon black pepper
2 tablespoons flour
1½ cups chicken broth
½ cup sherry

1. Heat butter in a large skillet. Place chicken pieces, skin side down, in skillet and brown on all sides.
2. Meanwhile, pour a mixture of vinegar and water over the mushrooms. Let stand 10 minutes; drain.
3. When chicken is evenly browned, transfer pieces to a shallow baking dish. Sprinkle the seasonings over the chicken. Spoon drained mushrooms over the top; sprinkle evenly with flour. Pour broth and wine over all.
4. Bake at 325°F about 1 hour, or until tender.

About 4 servings

Roast Turkey with Herbed Stuffing

Cooked Giblets and Broth
4 quarts ½-inch enriched bread
    cubes
1 cup snipped parsley
2 to 2½ teaspoons salt
2 teaspoons thyme
2 teaspoons rosemary, crushed
2 teaspoons marjoram
1 teaspoon ground sage
1 cup butter or margarine
1 cup coarsely chopped onion
1 cup coarsely chopped celery with
    leaves
1 turkey (14 to 15 pounds)
    Fat
3 tablespoons flour
¼ teaspoon salt
⅛ teaspoon ground black pepper

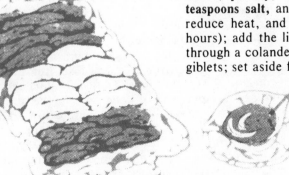

1. Prepare Cooked Giblets and Broth. Measure 1 cup chopped cooked giblets; set the broth aside.
2. Combine bread cubes, reserved giblets, and parsley in a large bowl. Blend salt, thyme, rosemary, marjoram, and sage; add to bread mixture and toss to mix.
3. Heat butter in a skillet. Mix in onion and celery; cook about 5 minutes, stirring occasionally. Toss with the bread mixture.
4. Add 1 to 2 cups broth (depending upon how moist a stuffing is desired), mixing lightly until ingredients are thoroughly blended.
5. Rinse turkey with cold water; pat dry, inside and out, with absorbent paper. Lightly fill body and neck cavities with the stuffing. Fasten neck skin to back with a skewer. Bring wing tips onto back of bird. Push drumsticks under band of skin at tail, if present, or tie to tail with cord.
6. Place turkey, breast side up, on rack in a shallow roasting pan. Brush skin with fat. Insert meat thermometer in the thickest part of the inner thigh muscle, being sure that tip does not touch bone.
7. Roast in a 325°F oven about 5 hours, or until thermometer registers 180° to 185°F. If desired, baste or brush bird occasionally with pan drippings. Place turkey on a heated platter; for easier carving, allow turkey to stand about 30 minutes.
8. Meanwhile, leaving brown residue in roasting pan, pour remaining drippings and fat into a bowl. Allow fat to rise to surface; skim off fat and measure 3 tablespoons into roasting pan. Blend flour, salt, and pepper with fat. Cook and stir until bubbly. Continue to stir while slowly adding 2 cups reserved liquid (broth and drippings). Cook, stirring constantly, until gravy thickens; scrape pan to blend in brown residue. Cook 1 to 2 minutes. If desired, mix in finely chopped cooked giblets the last few minutes of cooking.

About 25 servings

Cooked Giblets and Broth: Put **turkey neck** and **giblets** (except liver) into a saucepan with **1 large onion,** sliced, **parsley, celery with leaves, 1 medium bay leaf, 2 teaspoons salt,** and **1 quart water.** Cover, bring to boiling, reduce heat, and simmer until giblets are tender (about 2 hours); add the liver the last 15 minutes of cooking. Strain through a colander or sieve; reserve broth for stuffing. Chop giblets; set aside for stuffing and gravy.

Turkey-Oyster Casserole

1 tablespoon butter
2 teaspoons grated onion
4 ounces mushrooms, sliced
   lengthwise
¼ cup butter
¼ cup enriched all-purpose flour
1 teaspoon salt
¼ teaspoon ground pepper
Few grains cayenne pepper
2 cups milk
1 egg yolk, slightly beaten
2 tablespoons chopped parsley
¼ teaspoon thyme
2 drops Tabasco
1 pint oysters (with liquor)
2 cups diced cooked turkey
Buttered soft enriched bread
   crumbs

1. Heat 1 tablespoon butter with onion in a skillet; add mushrooms and cook over medium heat until lightly browned, stirring occasionally. Set aside.
2. Heat ¼ cup butter in a saucepan over low heat. Stir in flour, salt, pepper, and cayenne; cook until bubbly. Add milk gradually, stirring until well blended. Bring rapidly to boiling and boil 1 to 2 minutes, stirring constantly.
3. Blend a small amount of the hot sauce into egg yolk and return to remaining sauce, stirring until mixed. Stir in parsley, thyme, and Tabasco.
4. Heat oysters just to boiling; drain. Add oysters, turkey, and the mushrooms to sauce; toss lightly until thoroughly mixed.
5. Turn mixture into a buttered shallow 1½-quart baking dish. Sprinkle with crumbs.
6. Heat in a 400°F oven about 10 minutes, or until mixture is bubbly around edges and crumbs are golden brown.

About 6 servings

Roast Goose with Rice-and-Pickle Stuffing

3 cups cooked rice; or 1 package (6 ounces) seasoned white and wild rice mix, cooked following package directions
1 package (7 ounces) herb-seasoned stuffing croutons
2 medium navel oranges, pared and sectioned
2 onions, chopped
1 cup cranberries, rinsed, sorted, and chopped
1 cup sweet mixed pickles, drained and chopped
¼ cup sweet pickle liquid
½ to ¾ cup butter or margarine, melted
2 tablespoons brown sugar
1 goose (8 to 10 pounds)
1 tablespoon salt
¼ teaspoon ground black pepper
2 tablespoons light corn syrup
1½ cups orange juice
½ cup orange marmalade

1. Combine rice, stuffing croutons, orange sections, onions, cranberries, pickles and liquid, butter, and brown sugar in a large bowl; toss lightly until blended.
2. Rinse goose and remove any large layers of fat from the body cavity. Pat dry with absorbent paper. Rub body and neck cavities with salt and pepper.
3. Lightly spoon stuffing into the neck and body cavities. Overlap neck cavity with the skin and skewer to back of goose. Close body cavity with skewers and lace with cord. Loop cord around legs; tighten slightly and tie to a skewer inserted in the back above tail. Rub skin of goose with a little salt, if desired.
4. Put remaining stuffing into a greased casserole and cover; or cook in heavy-duty aluminum foil. Set in oven with goose during final hour of roasting.
5. Place goose, breast side down, on a rack in a large shallow roasting pan.
6. Roast in a 325°F oven 2 hours, removing fat from pan several times during this period.
7. Turn goose, breast side up. Blend corn syrup and 1 cup orange juice. Brush generously over goose. Roast about 1½ hours, or until goose tests done. To test for doneness, move leg gently by grasping end of bone; when done, drumstick-thigh joint moves easily or twists out. Brush frequently during final roasting period with the orange-syrup blend.
8. Transfer goose to a heated serving platter. Spoon 2 tablespoons drippings, the remaining ½ cup orange juice, and marmalade into a small saucepan. Heat thoroughly, stirring to blend. Pour into a serving dish or gravy boat to accompany goose.

6 to 8 servings

Rock Cornish Hens with Fruited Stuffing

1½ cups herb-seasoned stuffing
    croutons
½ cup drained canned apricot
    halves, cut in pieces
½ cup quartered seedless green
    grapes
⅓ cup chopped pecans
¼ cup butter or margarine, melted
2 tablespoons apricot nectar
1 tablespoon chopped parsley
¼ teaspoon salt
4 Rock Cornish hens (1 to 1½
    pounds each), thawed if
    purchased frozen
  Salt and pepper
⅓ cup apricot nectar
2 teaspoons soy sauce

1. Combine stuffing croutons, apricots, grapes, pecans, 2 tablespoons butter, 2 tablespoons apricot nectar, parsley, and ¼ teaspoon salt in a bowl; mix lightly.
2. Sprinkle cavities of hens with salt and pepper. Fill each hen with about ½ cup stuffing; fasten with skewers and lace with cord.
3. Blend ⅓ cup apricot nectar, soy sauce, and remaining butter. Place hens, breast side up, on a rack in a shallow roasting pan; brush generously with sauce.
4. Roast in a 350°F oven about 1½ hours, or until hens are tender and well browned; baste occasionally with sauce during roasting.

4 servings

Canard à l'Orange
(Roast Duckling with Orange Sauce)

2 ducklings (4 to 5 pounds each)
2 teaspoons salt
½ teaspoon pepper
1 clove garlic, peeled and cut
    crosswise into halves
½ cup dry white wine
½ cup orange marmalade
Sauce:
2 tablespoons butter or margarine
1 can (13¾ ounces) condensed
    chicken broth
½ cup orange marmalade
¼ cup dry white wine
¼ cup orange juice
2 teaspoons cornstarch
2 teaspoons lemon juice
2 tablespoons slivered orange peel

1. If frozen, let ducklings thaw according to package directions. Remove giblets, necks, and livers from ducklings. Reserve livers for sauce; if desired, reserve giblets and necks for soup stock. Remove and discard excess fat. Wash, drain, and pat dry with paper toweling. Rub cavities with salt, pepper, and garlic. Fasten neck skin of each to back with a skewer. Tuck tail ends into cavities. Tie legs together and tuck wing tips under ducklings. Prick skin generously to release fat. Place ducklings, breast side up, on a rack in a large shallow roasting pan.
2. Roast at 350°F 2 to 2½ hours or until legs can be moved easily, basting several times during roasting and removing accumulated drippings about every 30 minutes. Remove ducklings from oven and spread surface with mixture of wine and marmalade. Return to oven and continue roasting for 10 minutes.
3. For sauce, melt butter in a skillet. Add duckling livers and sauté until lightly browned. Remove and chop livers. Add chicken broth, marmalade, wine, orange juice, and cornstarch blended with lemon juice. Cook, stirring constantly over low heat for 10 minutes or until sauce bubbles and thickens. Stir in chopped livers and orange peel.
4. Transfer ducklings to a heated platter. Remove skewers and twine. Garnish, if desired, with watercress and orange slices. Reheat sauce if necessary and serve with duckling.

8 servings

SEAFOOD

Trout Amandine with Pineapple

6 whole trout
Lemon juice
Enriched all-purpose flour
6 tablespoons butter or margarine
Salt and pepper
2 tablespoons butter or margarine
½ cup slivered blanched almonds
6 well-drained canned pineapple
   slices
Paprika
Lemon wedges

1. Rinse trout quickly under running cold water; dry thoroughly. Brush trout inside and out with lemon juice. Coat with flour.
2. Heat 6 tablespoons butter in a large skillet. Add trout and brown on both sides. Season with salt and pepper.
3. Meanwhile, heat 2 tablespoons butter in another skillet over low heat. Add almonds and stir occasionally until golden.
4. Sprinkle pineapple slices with paprika. Place pineapple in skillet with almonds and brown lightly on both sides. Arrange trout on a warm serving platter and top with pineapple slices and almonds. Garnish platter with lemon wedges.

6 servings

Planked Halibut Dinner

4 halibut steaks, fresh or thawed
   frozen (about 2 pounds)
¼ cup butter, melted
2 tablespoons olive oil
1 tablespoon wine vinegar
2 teaspoons lemon juice
1 clove garlic, minced
¼ teaspoon dry mustard
¼ teaspoon marjoram
½ teaspoon salt
⅛ teaspoon ground black pepper
2 large zucchini
1 package (10 ounces) frozen green
   peas
1 can (8¼ ounces) tiny whole carrots
Au Gratin Potato Puffs
Butter
Fresh parsley
Lemon wedges

1. Place halibut steaks in an oiled baking pan.
2. Combine butter, olive oil, vinegar, lemon juice, garlic, dry mustard, marjoram, salt, and pepper. Drizzle over halibut.
3. Bake at 450°F 10 to 12 minutes, or until halibut is almost done.
4. Meanwhile, halve zucchini lengthwise and scoop out center portion. Cook in boiling salted water until just tender.
5. Cook peas following directions on package. Heat carrots.
6. Prepare Au Gratin Potato Puffs.
7. Arrange halibut on wooden plank or heated ovenware platter and border with zucchini halves filled with peas, carrots, and potato puffs. Dot peas and carrots with butter.
8. Place platter under broiler to brown potato puffs. Sprinkle carrots with chopped parsley.
9. Garnish with sprigs of parsley and lemon wedges arranged on a skewer.

4 servings

Au Gratin Potato Puffs: Pare 1½ **pounds potatoes;** cook and mash potatoes in a saucepan. Add **2 tablespoons butter** and ⅓ **cup milk;** whip until fluffy. Add **2 slightly beaten egg yolks, ½ cup shredded sharp Cheddar cheese, 1 teaspoon salt,** and **few grains pepper;** continue whipping. Using a pastry bag with a large star tip, form mounds about 2 inches in diameter on plank. Proceed as directed in recipe.

Canard a l'Orange 63
Petits Pois in Rice Ring 3

Baked Fish with Shrimp Stuffing

1 dressed whitefish, bass, or lake
    trout (2 to 3 pounds)
    Salt
1 cup chopped cooked shrimp
1 cup chopped fresh mushrooms
1 cup soft enriched bread crumbs
½ cup chopped celery
¼ cup chopped onion
2 tablespoons chopped parsley
¾ teaspoon salt
    Few grains black pepper
½ teaspoon thyme
¼ cup butter or margarine, melted
2 to 3 tablespoons apple cider
2 tablespoons butter or margarine,
    melted
    Parsley sprigs

1. Rinse fish under running cold water; drain well and pat dry with absorbent paper. Sprinkle fish cavity generously with salt.
2. Combine in a bowl the shrimp, mushrooms, bread crumbs, celery, onion, parsley, salt, pepper, and thyme. Pour ¼ cup melted butter gradually over bread mixture, tossing lightly until mixed.
3. Pile stuffing lightly into fish. Fasten with skewers and lace with cord. Place fish in a greased large shallow baking pan. Mix cider and 2 tablespoons melted butter; brush over fish.
4. Bake at 375°F, brushing occasionally with cider mixture, 25 to 30 minutes, or until fish flakes easily when pierced with a fork. If additional browning is desired, place fish under broiler 3 to 5 minutes. Transfer to a heated platter and remove skewers and cord. Garnish platter with parsley.

4 to 6 servings

California Style Red Snapper Steaks

6 fresh or thawed frozen red snapper
    steaks (about 2 pounds)
    Salt and pepper
¼ cup butter or margarine, melted
1 tablespoon grated orange peel
¼ cup orange juice
1 teaspoon lemon juice
    Dash nutmeg
    Fresh orange sections

1. Arrange red snapper steaks in a single layer in a well-greased baking pan; season with salt and pepper.
2. Combine butter, orange peel and juice, lemon juice, and nutmeg; pour over fish.
3. Bake at 350°F 20 to 25 minutes, or until fish flakes easily when tested with a fork.
4. To serve, put steaks onto a warm platter; spoon sauce in pan over them. Garnish with orange sections.

6 servings

Sole with Tangerine Sauce

1 pound sole fillets
5 tablespoons butter or margarine
2 teaspoons finely shredded tangerine
    peel
½ cup tangerine juice
1 teaspoon lemon juice
1 tablespoon finely chopped parsley
1 tablespoon finely chopped green
    onion
1 bay leaf
1 tangerine, peeled, sectioned, and
    seeds removed
3 tablespoons flour
½ teaspoon salt
⅛ teaspoon ground black pepper
3 tablespoons butter or margarine
    Parsley

1. Thaw fish if frozen.
2. Combine 5 tablespoons butter, tangerine peel and juice, lemon juice, 1 tablespoon parsley, green onion, and bay leaf in a saucepan. Bring to boiling and simmer over low heat until slightly thickened, stirring occasionally. Remove from heat; remove bay leaf and mix in tangerine sections. Keep sauce hot.
3. Mix flour, salt, and pepper; coat fish fillets. Heat 3 tablespoons butter in a skillet. Add fillets and fry until both sides are browned and fish flakes easily when tested with a fork.
4. Arrange fish on a hot platter and pour the hot sauce over it. Garnish with parsley.

About 4 servings

Glazed Apple Tart 78

Two-Layer Salmon-Rice Loaf

Salmon layer:
  1 **can (16 ounces) salmon**
  2 **cups coarse soft enriched bread**
     crumbs
  2 **tablespoons finely chopped onion**
  ½ **cup undiluted evaporated milk**
  1 **egg, slightly beaten**
  2 **tablespoons butter or margarine,**
     melted
  1 **tablespoon lemon juice**
  1 **teaspoon salt**

Rice layer:
  3 **cups cooked enriched rice**
  ¼ **cup finely chopped parsley**
  2 **eggs, slightly beaten**
  ⅔ **cup undiluted evaporated milk**
  2 **tablespoons butter or margarine,**
     melted
  ¼ **teaspoon salt**

Sauce:
  1 **large onion, quartered and thinly**
     sliced
  ¾ **cup water**
  1 **can (10¾ ounces) condensed**
     tomato soup

1. For salmon layer, drain salmon and remove skin. Flake salmon and put into a bowl. Add bread crumbs, onion, evaporated milk, egg, butter, lemon juice, and salt; mix lightly. Turn into a buttered 9×5×3-inch loaf pan; press lightly to form a layer.
2. For rice layer, combine rice with parsley, eggs, evaporated milk, butter, and salt. Spoon over salmon layer; press lightly.
3. Set filled loaf pan in a shallow pan. Pour hot water into pan to a depth of 1 inch.
4. Bake at 375°F about 45 minutes. Remove from water immediately.
5. Meanwhile, for sauce, put onion and water into a saucepan. Bring to boiling, reduce heat, and simmer, covered, 10 minutes. Remove onion, if desired. Add condensed soup to saucepan, stir until blended, and bring to boiling.
6. Cut loaf into slices and top servings with tomato sauce.

About 8 servings

Broiled Salmon

  6 **salmon steaks, cut ½ inch thick**
  1 **cup sauterne**
  ½ **cup vegetable oil**
  2 **tablespoons wine vinegar**
  2 **teaspoons soy sauce**
  2 **tablespoons chopped green onion**
    Seasoned salt
    Green onion, chopped (optional)
    Pimento strips (optional)

1. Put salmon steaks into a large shallow dish. Mix sauterne, oil, wine vinegar, soy sauce, and green onion; pour over salmon. Marinate in refrigerator several hours or overnight, turning occasionally.
2. To broil, remove steaks from marinade and place on broiler rack. Set under broiler with top 6 inches from heat. Broil about 5 minutes on each side, brushing generously with marinade several times. About 2 minutes before removing from broiler, sprinkle each steak lightly with seasoned salt and, if desired, top with green onion and pimento. Serve at once.

6 servings

Broiled Trout

  Trout (8- to 10-ounce fish for each
    serving)
  French dressing
  Instant minced onion
  Salt

1. Remove head and fins from trout, if desired. Rinse trout quickly under running cold water; dry thoroughly. Brush inside of fish with French dressing and sprinkle generously with instant minced onion and salt. Brush outside generously with French dressing.

Tuna Fiesta

1 can (6½ or 7 ounces) tuna, drained
    and separated in large pieces
1 can (16 ounces) stewed tomatoes,
    drained
1 can (15¼ ounces) spaghetti in
    tomato sauce with cheese
1 tablespoon ketchup
1 teaspoon seasoned salt
½ cup (about 2 ounces) shredded
    sharp Cheddar cheese
    Few grains paprika
    Fresh parsley

1. Turn tuna, stewed tomatoes, and spaghetti into a saucepan. Add ketchup, seasoned salt, cheese, and paprika; mix well. Set over medium heat, stirring occasionally, until thoroughly heated (about 8 minutes).
2. Turn into a warm serving dish; garnish with parsley. Serve at once.

About 6 servings

Note: If desired, reserve cheese and paprika for topping. Mix remaining ingredients and turn into a greased 1-quart casserole. Top with the cheese and paprika. Set in a 350°F oven 20 minutes, or until thoroughly heated. Garnish with parsley.

Patio Crab Casserole

¼ cup butter or margarine
2 cups chopped onion
1 pound frozen or 2 cans (7½
    ounces each) Alaska king crab,
    drained and sliced
½ cup snipped parsley
2 tablespoons capers
2 tablespoons snipped chives
2 pimentos, diced
1½ cups corn muffin mix
⅛ teaspoon salt
1 egg, fork beaten
½ cup milk
1 cup cream-style golden corn
6 drops Tabasco
2 cups dairy sour cream
1½ cups shredded extra sharp
    Cheddar cheese

1. Heat butter in a skillet. Add onion and cook until tender. Stir in crab, parsley, capers, chives, and pimentos; heat.
2. Meanwhile, stir corn muffin mix, salt, egg, milk, corn, and Tabasco until just moistened (batter should be lumpy). Turn into a greased shallow 3-quart dish and spread evenly to edges.
3. Spoon crab mixture and then sour cream over batter. Sprinkle cheese over all.
4. Bake at 400°F 25 to 30 minutes.
5. To serve, cut into squares.

About 12 servings

Savory Oysters

⅓ cup butter or margarine
1 can (4 ounces) sliced mushrooms,
    drained
⅓ cup chopped green pepper
½ clove garlic
2 cups coarse toasted enriched bread
    crumbs
1 quart oysters, drained (reserve
    liquor)
¼ cup cream
1 teaspoon Worcestershire sauce
1 teaspoon salt
1 teaspoon paprika
⅛ teaspoon ground mace
    Few grains cayenne pepper

1. Heat butter in a large skillet. Add mushrooms, green pepper, and garlic; cook about 5 minutes. Remove skillet from heat; discard garlic. Stir in toasted bread crumbs. Set aside.
2. Mix ¼ cup reserved oyster liquor, cream, and Worcestershire sauce.
3. Blend salt, paprika, mace, and cayenne.
4. Use about a third of crumb mixture to form a layer in bottom of a greased 2-quart casserole. Arrange about half of oysters and half of seasonings over crumbs. Repeat crumb layer, then oyster and seasoning layers. Pour the liquid mixture over all. Top with remaining crumbs.
5. Bake at 375°F 20 to 30 minutes, or until thoroughly heated and crumbs are golden brown.

6 to 8 servings

Mock Lobster, Flemish Style

The main ingredient in this dish is monk fish, which has a taste and texture somewhat similar to lobster. Served in scallop shells or ramekins, it makes a delectable fish course during a multiple-course dinner

1 **pound monk fish fillets**
1 **can or bottle (12 ounces) beer**
½ **cup water**
1 **small onion, quartered**
1 **small celery stalk with top, cut in chunks**
½ **teaspoon salt**
¼ **teaspoon thyme**
2 **tablespoons butter or margarine**
2 **tablespoons flour**
¼ **cup cream**
1 **egg yolk**
½ **cup shredded cheese (Edam, Gruyère, Cheddar)**

1. Cut fish fillets in half lengthwise; then cut each section into ¾-inch slices.
2. In a large saucepan, place beer, water, onion, celery, salt, and thyme. Heat to boiling. Add fish. Cover and simmer 4 minutes, or until fish flakes.
3. Remove fish with a slotted spoon. Drain well on paper towels. Boil stock 10 minutes to reduce; strain.
4. In another saucepan, melt butter. Stir in flour. Add ¾ cup strained stock and the cream. Cook, stirring constantly, until thickened.
5. Add a little hot mixture to egg yolk; return to pan. Cook slowly, stirring, 1 to 2 minutes. Remove from heat; adjust seasonings.
6. Gently combine fish and sauce. Spoon into scallop shells or individual ramekins. Sprinkle with cheese. Broil 2 minutes, or just until tops are lightly browned.

6 appetizer servings

Saucy Fish Fillets

This delicately flavored entrée consists of fish poached in beer and a hollandaise-style sauce with egg yolks, cream, butter, and part of the cooking liquid.

1 **pound fish fillets**
1 **can or bottle (12 ounces) beer**
1 **small onion, quartered**
1 **celery stalk, cut in chunks**
2 **tablespoons minced fresh parsley or 1 tablespoon dried parsley flakes**
1 **teaspoon salt**
Dash white pepper
2 **egg yolks**
2 **tablespoons cream**
2 **tablespoons butter or margarine**

1. Thaw fish, if frozen.
2. Put beer, onion, celery, parsley, salt, and pepper in a skillet. Heat to boiling. Add fish. Cover and simmer about 8 to 10 minutes, or just until fish flakes with a fork.
3. Drain fish and put onto a deep platter. Place in a 300°F oven to keep warm. Boil cooking liquid about 5 minutes to reduce; strain.
4. In top of a double boiler, beat egg yolks with cream. Gradually stir in ½ cup hot strained cooking liquid. Cook over boiling water, stirring constantly, until thickened. Cut butter into small pieces; stir into sauce, one piece at a time. Pour sauce over fish. (Recipe makes about ¾ cup sauce.)

3 or 4 servings

Baked Salmon Squares

1 can (15½ ounces) salmon, drained
  and flaked
½ cup fine dry bread crumbs
1 can (10¾ ounces) condensed cream
  of celery soup
¼ cup dairy sour cream
2 eggs, beaten

1. Combine all ingredients. Put into a greased 8-inch square baking dish.
2. Bake, uncovered, at 325°F 1 hour, or until set. Cut into squares and serve with **creamed spinach.**

6 servings

Shrimp and Rice Supreme

1 medium onion, thinly sliced
⅓ cup chopped green pepper
½ cup sliced fresh mushrooms
¼ cup butter or margarine
¼ cup flour
½ teaspoon salt
  Dash ground red pepper
2 cups milk
1 tablespoon Worcestershire sauce
2 cups cooked white rice
1 pound cooked and cleaned shrimp

1. Sauté onion, green pepper, and mushrooms in butter in a skillet. Stir in flour, salt, and red pepper. Gradually add milk, stirring until thickened and smooth.
2. Combine sauce with remaining ingredients. Put into a 2-quart casserole.
3. Bake, covered, at 350°F 30 minutes, or until bubbly.

6 servings

Shrimp Florentine

1 package (10 ounces) frozen spinach,
  cooked and squeezed
1 pound cooked and cleaned shrimp
1 can (10¾ ounces) condensed cream
  of chicken soup
¼ cup sherry
1 tablespoon snipped parsley
  Dash pepper
½ cup (2 ounces) shredded Cheddar
  cheese
¼ cup buttered bread crumbs

1. Put spinach into a 1½-quart casserole.
2. Blend shrimp, soup, sherry, parsley, and pepper. Spoon over spinach.
3. Combine cheese and crumbs. Sprinkle over all.
4. Bake, covered, at 350°F 30 minutes, or until heated through.

4 servings

Fish Stew with Red Wine

2 pounds fish
2 cups red wine
1 carrot, sliced
1 onion, minced
2 cloves garlic, cut in halves
1 teaspoon salt
¼ teaspoon pepper
Herb Bouquet
3 tablespoons brandy
3 tablespoons melted butter
2 tablespoons all-purpose flour

1. Set out a deep heavy skillet with a tight-fitting cover.
2. Clean, wash, dry, and cut fish into thick slices. Put fish into skillet and add wine, carrot, onion, garlic, salt, pepper, and Herb Bouquet; bring to boiling.
3. Heat brandy in a small saucepan. Ignite brandy and immediately pour over the fish. When the flame has burned out, cover the pan. Cook fish slowly 15 to 20 minutes, or until the fish flakes when pierced with a fork. Remove fish to a warm serving dish. Keep hot. Strain and reserve cooking liquid.
4. Blend thoroughly in same skillet butter and flour. Cook over low heat until mixture bubbles. Remove from heat; gradually stir in cooking liquid. Cook rapidly; stir constantly until sauce thickens. Boil 1 to 2 minutes longer. Pour sauce over the fish.
5. Serve with **garlic croutons.** Garnish with **tiny cooked onions, sautéed mushrooms,** or **cooked shrimp.**

4 servings

Herb Bouquet: Tie together neatly **3 or 4 sprigs of parsley, 1 sprig thyme,** and ½ **bay leaf.** If dry herbs are used, enclose in fine cheesecloth bag.

Mussels Cooked in Wine Sauce

2 quarts mussels
2 cups dry white wine such as chablis
1 cup finely chopped shallots
½ cup finely chopped parsley
⅓ cup unsalted butter
Freshly ground white pepper
Juice of ½ lemon
Salt
Hollandaise Sauce:
2 egg yolks
2 tablespoons cream

1. Scrub mussels under running water and trim off the beards.
2. Pour wine over mussels in a saucepot; add shallots, parsley, butter, and white pepper to taste. Cover tightly and cook over high heat about 2 minutes; stir the mixture and cook, covered, 2 minutes longer, or until mussel shells open.
3. Remove the mussels from saucepot; remove and discard top shells, placing the filled bottom shells in a serving dish. Keep warm.
4. Cook the pan juice over high heat to reduce the amount by one half. Remove from heat. Add lemon juice, salt, and white pepper to taste.
5. For hollandaise sauce, in the top of a double boiler, beat egg

¼ teaspoon salt
Few grains cayenne pepper
2 tablespoons lemon juice or
tarragon vinegar
½ cup butter

yolks, cream, salt, and cayenne pepper until thick with a whisk beater. Set over hot (not boiling) water. (Bottom of double-boiler top should not touch water.)

6. Add the lemon juice gradually, while beating constantly. Cook, beating constantly with the whisk beater, until sauce is the consistency of thick cream. Remove double boiler from heat, leaving top in place.

7. Beating constantly, add the butter, ½ teaspoon at a time. Beat with whisk beater until butter is melted and thoroughly blended in. Mix with wine sauce.

8. Pour the sauce over the mussels and serve immediately.

4 servings

Scallops Baked in Shells

2 cups dry white wine
Herb Bouquet
2 pounds (1 quart) scallops
½ teaspoon salt
½ pound mushrooms
6 shallots or ¼ cup minced onions
1 tablespoon minced parsley
3 tablespoons butter
2 tablespoons water
1 teaspoon lemon juice
¼ cup melted butter
¼ cup all-purpose flour
2 egg yolks, slightly beaten
¼ cup heavy cream
⅓ cup buttered dry bread crumbs

1. Butter 6 baking shells or ramekins.
2. Heat wine in a saucepan with Herb Bouquet.
3. Wash scallops in cold water and drain.
4. Add scallops and salt to wine, cover and simmer about 10 minutes, or until tender. Remove Herb Bouquet, drain scallops, and reserve the liquid. Cut scallops into fine pieces and set aside.
5. Clean and chop mushrooms.
6. Add mushrooms, shallots, parsley, butter, water, and lemon juice to a saucepan; cover and simmer 5 to 10 minutes. Strain liquid into seasoned wine. Add vegetable mixture to scallops. Set aside.
7. Make a roux by blending butter and flour in a saucepan. Cook over low heat until mixture bubbles. Remove from heat and gradually stir in wine and vegetable liquid. Return to heat and bring rapidly to boiling, stirring constantly; cook 1 to 2 minutes longer.
8. Remove sauce from heat and add egg yolks and cream gradually, stirring vigorously. Then stir in the scallop mixture.
9. Fill shells or ramekins, piling high in center. Sprinkle with about ⅓ cup of buttered bread crumbs.
10. To brown, set shells on a baking sheet and place in oven at 450°F 8 to 10 minutes, or place under broiler 3 to 4 minutes from heat to top of the creamed mixture. Serve when browned.

6 servings

Herb Bouquet: Tie neatly together **3 or 4 sprigs of parsley, 1 sprig thyme,** and **½ bay leaf.** If dry herbs are used, enclose in fine cheesecloth bag.

DESSERTS

Peaches 'n' Corn Bread, Shortcake Style

1 cup sifted enriched all-purpose
    flour
½ teaspoon baking soda
¼ teaspoon salt
1 cup enriched yellow cornmeal
¾ cup firmly packed light brown
    sugar
1 egg, beaten
½ cup buttermilk
⅓ cup dairy sour cream
    Peach Butter Elégante
    Sweetened fresh peach slices

1. Blend flour, baking soda, salt, cornmeal, and brown sugar in a bowl; set aside.
2. Beat egg, buttermilk, and sour cream until well blended; add to dry ingredients and stir until just smooth (do not overmix).
3. Turn into a greased 11×7×1½-inch pan and spread batter evenly.
4. Bake at 425°F about 20 minutes.
5. While still warm, cut corn bread into serving-size pieces, remove from pan, and split into two layers. Spread Peach Butter Elégante generously between layers. Top with peach slices.

9 or 12 servings

Peach Butter Elégante: Thaw **1 package (10 or 12 ounces) frozen sliced peaches.** Drain peaches and cut into pieces; set aside. Put **1 cup firm unsalted butter** or **1 cup margarine** into a small mixing bowl. Beat with electric mixer on high speed just until butter is whipped. Add **½ cup confectioners' sugar** gradually, beating thoroughly. Add the peaches, about 1 tablespoon at a time, beating thoroughly after each addition. (Do not allow butter to become too soft.) Chill until ready to use.

About 2 cups peach butter

Spicy Peach Cobbler

1 can (29 ounces) sliced peaches,
    drained; reserve 1 cup syrup
½ cup firmly packed brown sugar
2 tablespoons cornstarch
⅛ teaspoon salt
⅛ teaspoon ground cinnamon
⅛ teaspoon ground cloves
2 tablespoons cider vinegar
1 tablespoon butter or margarine
1 cup all-purpose biscuit mix
½ cup finely shredded sharp Cheddar
    cheese
2 tablespoons butter or margarine,
    melted
¼ cup milk

1. Put drained peaches into a shallow 1-quart baking dish. Set aside.
2. Mix brown sugar, cornstarch, salt, cinnamon, and cloves in a saucepan. Blend in reserved peach syrup and vinegar; add 1 tablespoon butter. Bring mixture to boiling, stirring frequently; cook until thickened, about 10 minutes. Pour over peaches and set in a 400°F oven.
3. Combine biscuit mix and cheese. Stir in melted butter and milk to form a soft dough. Remove dish from oven and drop dough by heaping tablespoonfuls on top of hot peaches.
4. Return to oven and bake 20 minutes, or until crust is golden brown. Serve warm.

6 servings

Cantaloupe Sherbet

2 cups ripe cantaloupe pieces
1 egg white
½ cup sugar
2 tablespoons fresh lime juice

1. Put melon pieces, egg white, sugar, and lime juice into an electric blender container. Cover and blend until smooth.
2. Turn into a shallow baking dish. Set in freezer; stir occasionally during freezing.
3. To serve, spoon into chilled dessert dishes.

About 1½ pints sherbet

Pineapple Sherbet: Follow recipe for Cantaloupe Sherbet; substitute **2 cups fresh pineapple pieces** for cantaloupe.

Watermelon Sherbet: Follow recipe for Cantaloupe Sherbet; substitute **2 cups watermelon pieces** for cantaloupe and, if desired, decrease sugar to ¼ cup.

Banana-Pineapple Ice Cream

2 cups mashed ripe bananas (about 5 medium)
1 cup sugar
1 teaspoon grated orange peel
1 teaspoon grated lemon peel
3 tablespoons lemon juice
2 tablespoons lime juice
1½ cups unsweetened pineapple juice
⅓ cup orange juice
2 cans (14½ ounces each) evaporated milk

1. Crushed ice and rock salt will be needed. Wash and scald cover, container, and dasher of a 3- or 4-quart ice cream freezer. Chill thoroughly.
2. Combine bananas, sugar, orange peel, lemon peel, lemon juice, and lime juice; blend thoroughly. Set aside about 10 minutes.
3. Stir fruit juices into banana mixture. Add evaporated milk gradually, stirring until well blended.
4. Fill chilled freezer container no more than two-thirds full with ice cream mixture. Cover tightly. Set into freezer tub. (For electric freezer, follow the directions.)
5. Fill tub with alternate layers of crushed ice and rock salt, using 8 parts ice to 1 part salt. Turn handle slowly 5 minutes. Then turn rapidly until handle becomes difficult to turn (about 15 minutes), adding ice and salt as necessary.
6. Wipe cover and remove dasher. Pack down ice cream and cover with waxed paper or plastic wrap. Replace lid. (Plug dasher opening unless freezer has a solid cover.) Repack freezer container in ice, using 4 parts ice to 1 part salt. Cover with heavy paper or cloth. Let ripen 2 hours.

About 2 quarts ice cream

Quick Applesauce Whip

1 can (16 ounces) applesauce
½ teaspoon grated lemon peel
2 teaspoons lemon juice
½ teaspoon ground cinnamon
3 egg whites
⅛ teaspoon salt
6 tablespoons sugar
Ground nutmeg

1. Combine applesauce, lemon peel, juice, and cinnamon.
2. Beat egg whites and salt until frothy. Add sugar gradually, beat well. Continue beating until rounded peaks are formed. Fold beaten egg whites into applesauce mixture.
3. Spoon immediately into dessert dishes. Sprinkle nutmeg over each serving.

About 6 servings

Date Spice Cake

2¼ cups sifted enriched all-purpose
    flour
2 teaspoons baking powder
¼ teaspoon baking soda
½ teaspoon salt
2 teaspoons ground nutmeg
2 teaspoons ground ginger
⅔ cup shortening
1 teaspoon grated orange peel
1 teaspoon grated lemon peel
1 cup sugar
2 eggs
1 cup buttermilk
1 cup chopped dates

1. Grease a 9×9×2-inch pan. Line with waxed paper cut to fit bottom; grease paper. Set aside.
2. Blend flour, baking powder, baking soda, salt, nutmeg, and ginger.
3. Beat shortening with orange and lemon peels. Add sugar gradually, creaming until fluffy after each addition.
4. Add eggs, one at a time, beating thoroughly after each addition.
5. Beating only until smooth after each addition, alternately add dry ingredients in fourths and buttermilk in thirds to creamed mixture. Mix in dates. Turn batter into prepared pan.
6. Bake at 350°F about 45 minutes.
7. Remove from oven. Cool 5 to 10 minutes in pan on wire rack. Remove cake from pan and peel off paper; cool cake on rack.

One 9-inch square cake

Carrot Cupcakes

1½ cups sifted enriched all-purpose
    flour
1 teaspoon baking powder
1 teaspoon baking soda
1 teaspoon ground cinnamon
½ teaspoon salt
1 cup sugar
¾ cup vegetable oil
2 eggs
1 cup grated raw carrots
½ cup chopped nuts

1. Blend flour, baking powder, baking soda, cinnamon, and salt. Set aside.
2. Combine sugar and oil in a bowl and beat thoroughly. Add eggs, one at a time, beating thoroughly after each addition. Mix in carrots. Add dry ingredients gradually, beating until blended. Mix in nuts.
3. Spoon into paper-baking-cup-lined muffin-pan wells.
4. Bake at 350°F 15 to 20 minutes.

About 16 cupcakes

Triple-Treat Walnut Bars

½ cup butter or margarine
1 package (3 ounces) cream cheese
½ cup firmly packed dark brown
    sugar
1 cup whole wheat flour
⅓ cup toasted wheat germ
1 package (6 ounces) semisweet
    chocolate pieces
2 eggs
½ cup honey
⅓ cup whole wheat flour
⅓ cup instant nonfat dry milk
¼ teaspoon salt
¼ teaspoon ground cinnamon
¼ teaspoon ground mace
1½ cups chopped walnuts

1. Cream butter, cheese, and sugar in a bowl until light. Add 1 cup whole wheat flour and wheat germ and mix until smooth. Turn into a greased 13×9×2-inch pan; spread evenly.
2. Bake at 375°F 15 to 18 minutes, until edges are very lightly browned and top is firm.
3. Remove from oven and sprinkle with chocolate. Let stand about 5 minutes, or until chocolate softens, then spread it evenly over baked layer.
4. Combine eggs and honey; beat just until well blended. Add ⅓ cup whole wheat flour, dry milk, salt, cinnamon, mace, and walnuts; mix well. Spoon over the chocolate.
5. Return to oven and bake 18 to 20 minutes, or until top is set. Cool in pan, then cut into bars or diamonds.

About 3 dozen cookies

Raisin-Nut Spice Cake

Serve this moist, dark, and delectable cake any time of year with whipped cream, ice cream, or Beer Dessert Sauce on top. It is delicious served warm with hard sauce during the holiday season.

3 cups sifted cake flour
2 teaspoons baking powder
1 teaspoon baking soda
½ teaspoon cinnamon
½ teaspoon nutmeg
¼ teaspoon ginger
¼ teaspoon salt
1 can or bottle (12 ounces) beer
1 cup raisins (5 ounces)
¾ cup butter or margarine
1 cup sugar
½ cup molasses
2 eggs
¾ cup chopped nuts (3 ounces)
Glaze

1. Sift dry ingredients together. Set aside.
2. Heat beer and raisins to simmering; let stand about 15 minutes to plump.
3. Cream butter and sugar until light and fluffy; add molasses.
4. Add eggs, one at a time, beating well after each addition.
5. Add dry ingredients alternately in thirds with beer drained from raisins, beating just until well blended. Stir in raisins and nuts.
6. Turn into a well-greased and floured 10-inch Bundt pan or angel food cake pan (nonstick pan preferred).
7. Bake at 350°F 1 hour, or until done.
8. Let stand in pan about 10 minutes; invert onto cake rack. Cool. Cover with foil or store in airtight container. Cake slices better if made a day in advance.
9. Prepare a glaze by thinning **1 cup sifted confectioners' sugar** with **beer** or **milk.** Drizzle over cake shortly before serving.

1 large cake; 16 servings

Old English Cheesecake

Raisins, almonds, lemon peel, and beer delectably perk up the flavor of this rich dessert.

Crust:
1¼ cups all-purpose flour
¼ cup sugar
⅓ cup butter or margarine
4 tablespoons cold beer

Filling:
½ cup golden raisins (2½ ounces), chopped
⅓ cup almonds (2 ounces), finely chopped
1 tablespoon grated lemon peel
1 pound cottage cheese
½ cup flour
4 eggs
1 cup sugar
¾ cup beer
⅛ teaspoon nutmeg

1. For crust, mix flour and sugar; cut in butter until crumbly. Add beer 1 tablespoon at a time, stirring with a fork. Shape dough into a ball. Chill.
2. Roll out on floured surface to a 13- to 14-inch circle. Fold in quarters. Gently unfold in a 9-inch springform pan. Even edge of crust so it extends about 2 inches up sides of pan (1½ inches up sides if using a 10-inch pan). Prick all over with fork.
3. Bake at 425°F 10 minutes. Prick again and press to sides. Bake 10 minutes more, or until slightly golden.
4. For filling, mix chopped raisins, almonds, and peel.
5. Process cottage cheese, flour, and eggs until smooth, using food processor or electric blender. (Do in several batches in blender.)
6. Add sugar, beer, and nutmeg; blend until smooth. Stir in raisin mixture. Pour into cooled shell.
7. Bake at 300°F 1¼ to 1½ hours, or until set. Cool to room temperature for serving. Dust with **confectioners' sugar** and top with **whole unblanched almonds.**

8 to 10 servings

Buttery Baked Apples

8 medium baking apples, cored
1 cup sugar
6 tablespoons butter or margarine
1 tablespoon cornstarch
1 tablespoon cold water
½ teaspoon vanilla extract
½ cup milk

1. Put apples into a 1½-quart baking dish. Sprinkle with sugar. Dot with butter.
2. Bake, uncovered, at 450°F 20 minutes, or until fork-tender, basting occasionally.
3. Remove baking dish from oven and apples from baking dish.
4. Combine cornstarch, water, and vanilla extract; add to milk. Stir into liquid in baking dish. Return apples to baking dish.
5. Bake an additional 8 to 10 minutes, or until sauce is thickened. To serve, spoon sauce over each apple.

8 servings

Cherry-Pineapple Cobbler

1 can (21 ounces) cherry pie filling
1 can (13¼ ounces) pineapple tidbits, drained
¼ teaspoon allspice
3 tablespoons honey
1 egg, slightly beaten
½ cup dairy sour cream
1½ cups unflavored croutons

1. Combine cherry pie filling, pineapple tidbits, allspice, and 1 tablespoon honey. Put into a 1½-quart baking dish.
2. Blend egg, sour cream, and remaining 2 tablespoons honey. Stir in croutons. Spoon over cherry-pineapple mixture.
3. Bake, uncovered, at 375°F 30 minutes, or until heated through. If desired, top with ice cream.

8 servings

Indian Pudding

3 cups milk
½ cup cornmeal
1 tablespoon butter or margarine
½ cup light molasses
½ teaspoon salt
½ teaspoon ginger
1 cup cold milk

1. Scald 2½ cups milk in top of double boiler over boiling water.
2. Combine cornmeal and the remaining ½ cup milk. Add to scalded milk, stirring constantly. Cook about 25 minutes, stirring frequently.
3. Stir in butter, molasses, salt, and ginger.
4. Pour into a greased 1½-quart baking dish. Pour the 1 cup cold milk over pudding.
5. Set in a baking pan. Pour boiling water around dish to within 1 inch of top.
6. Bake, covered, at 300°F about 2 hours. Remove cover and bake an additional 1 hour. Serve warm or cold with **cream** or **ice cream.**

6 servings

Chocolate Custard

1 package (6 ounces) semisweet
   chocolate pieces
3 tablespoons half-and-half
3 cups milk
3 eggs
1 teaspoon vanilla extract
⅓ cup sugar
¼ teaspoon salt

1. Melt 2/3 cup chocolate pieces with half-and-half in top of a double boiler over hot (not boiling) water. Stir until smooth; spoon about 1 tablespoon into each of 8 custard cups or 10 soufflé dishes. Spread evenly. Put cups into a shallow pan; set aside.
2. Scald milk. Melt remaining 1/3 cup chocolate pieces and, adding gradually, stir in scalded milk until blended.
3. Beat together eggs, vanilla extract, sugar, and salt. Gradually add milk mixture, stirring constantly. Pour into chocolate-lined cups.
4. Set pan with filled cups on oven rack and pour boiling water into pan to a depth of 1 inch.
5. Bake, uncovered, at 325°F 25 minutes, or until a knife inserted halfway between center and edge comes out clean.
6. Set cups on wire rack to cool slightly. Refrigerate and serve when thoroughly cooled. Unmold and, if desired, garnish with whipped cream rosettes.

8 to 10 servings

Brazilian Pudim Moka with Chocolate Sauce

3 cups milk
1 cup half-and-half
5 tablespoons instant coffee
2 teaspoons grated orange peel
4 eggs
1 egg yolk
½ cup sugar
½ teaspoon salt
1 teaspoon vanilla extract
  Nutmeg
  Chocolate sauce
  Chopped Brazil nuts

1. Combine milk and half-and-half in top of a double boiler and heat over simmering water until scalded.
2. Add instant coffee and orange peel, stirring until coffee is dissolved. Remove from simmering water and set aside to cool (about 10 minutes).
3. Beat together eggs and egg yolk slightly. Blend in sugar and salt.
4. Gradually add coffee mixture, stirring constantly. Mix in vanilla extract. Strain through a fine sieve into eight 6-ounce custard cups. Sprinkle with nutmeg. Set cups in pan of hot water.
5. Bake, uncovered, at 325°F 25 to 30 minutes, or until a knife inserted in center of custard comes out clean.
6. Cool and chill. To serve, invert onto serving plates. Pour chocolate sauce over top and sprinkle with Brazil nuts.

8 servings

Rosy Rhubarb Swirls

1½ cups sugar
1¼ cups water
⅓ cup red cinnamon candies
2 or 3 drops red food coloring
2¼ cups all-purpose flour
4 teaspoons baking powder
½ teaspoon salt
⅔ cup milk
⅓ cup half-and-half
3 cups finely diced fresh rhubarb (if
   tender do not peel)

1. Put sugar, water, and cinnamon candies into a saucepan. Stirring occasionally, cook over medium heat until candies are melted and mixture forms a thin syrup (about 10 minutes). Stir in food coloring.
2. Meanwhile, sift together into a bowl the flour, baking powder, and salt. Add a mixture of milk and half-and-half and stir with a fork only until dry ingredients are moistened. Turn onto a floured surface and knead lightly about 10 times with fingertips.
3. Roll dough into a 13x11x¼-inch rectangle. Spoon rhubarb evenly over dough. Beginning with longer side, roll dough and seal edges. Cut crosswise into 12 slices.
4. Pour syrup into a shallow baking dish and arrange rolls, cut side up, in syrup. Sprinkle with additional sugar (¼ to ⅓ cup) and top each roll with a small piece of **butter**.
5. Bake, uncovered, at 400°F 25 to 30 minutes. Serve warm with **half-and-half**.

12 servings

Glazed Apple Tart in Wheat Germ Crust

Wheat Germ Crust (see recipe)
8 medium apples
1 cup red port
1 cup water
⅓ cup honey
2 tablespoons lemon juice
⅛ teaspoon salt
3 drops red food coloring
1 package (8 ounces) cream
　　cheese
1 tablespoon half-and-half
1 tablespoon honey
1½ tablespoons cornstarch

1. Prepare crust and set aside to cool.
2. Pare, core, and cut apples into eighths to make 2 quarts.
3. Combine port, water, ⅓ cup honey, lemon juice, salt, and food coloring in large skillet with a cover. Add half the apples in single layer, cover, and cook slowly about 5 minutes, until apples are barely tender. Remove apples with slotted spoon and arrange in a single layer in a shallow pan. Cook remaining apples in same manner. Chill apples, saving cooking liquid for glaze.
4. Beat cream cheese with half-and-half and 1 tablespoon honey. Spread in even layer over bottom of cooled crust, saving about ¼ cup for decoration on top of tart, if desired.
5. Arrange apples over cheese.
6. Boil syrup from cooking apples down to 1 cup.
7. Mix cornstarch with 1½ tablespoons cold water. Stir into syrup, and cook, stirring, until mixture clears and thickens. Set pan in cold water, and cool quickly to room temperature. Spoon carefully over apples.
8. Chill until glaze is set before cutting.

One 10-inch tart

Wheat Germ Crust

1½ cups sifted all-purpose flour
3 tablespoons wheat germ
3 tablespoons packed brown
　　sugar
¾ teaspoon salt
⅛ teaspoon cinnamon
6 tablespoons shortening
2 tablespoons butter
2 tablespoons milk (about)

1. Combine flour, wheat germ, brown sugar, salt, and cinnamon in mixing bowl.
2. Cut in shortening and butter as for pie crust.
3. Sprinkle with just enough milk to make dough stick together.
4. Press dough against bottom and up sides of 10-inch springform pan to make shell 1¾ inches deep. Prick bottom. Set on baking sheet.
5. Bake at 375°F on lowest shelf of oven for about 20 minutes, or until golden.

INDEX

Apples, Buttery Baked 76
Applesauce Appetizers, Sausage and 5
Applesauce Whip, Quick 73
Artichoke Casserole, Spinach 42
Artichoke Hearts Supreme, Marinated 38
Asparagus, Butter-Sauced 35
Aspic, Stewed Tomato 11
Avocado Sandwiches on Sour Dough 7

Bacon-Bean Salad 9
Barley Italienne 34
Barley-Mushroom Casserole 34
Bars, Triple-Treat Walnut 74
Bean and Proscuitto Soup 17
Beef
   and Pea Casserole 47
   Bake, Easy Corned 49
   Bake, Oven 48
   Bourguignon 48
   Burgundy 49
   Stew Savory 46
   Swiss Steak Mozarella 48
   with Wine, Pot Roast of 49
Beets, Zesty 36
Bisque, Cool and Creamy Shrimp and Avocado 20
Bisque, Creamy Shrimp and Avocado 20
Black Bread, Peasant 28
Bouillabaisse 21
Braided Egg Bread 23
Brazilian Pudim Moka with Chocolate Sauce 77
Broccoli
   Bake 39
   Mushroom Casserole 39
   Scalloped Corn and 40
   Soup, Cream of 18
   with Buttery Lemon Crunch 35
Brussels Sprouts in Broth 39
Brussels Sprouts in Herb Butter 35

Cabbage
   Casserole 40
   Rolls Paprikash 36
   Soup, Chinese 18
Cake, Date Spice 74
Cake, Raisin-Nut Spice 75
Canapés, Wine-Cheese 6
Canard à l'Orange 63
Carrot Spread, Baked 5
Carrots, Brandied 40
Casserole
   Barley-Mushroom 34
   Bavarian 52
   Beef and Pea 47
   Broccoli-Mushroom 39
   Cabbage 40
   Chicken and Tomato 59

Italian Rice 31
   Layered 38
   Layered Ham and Noodle 53
   Mushroom-Rice 31
   Spinach-Artichoke 42
   Turkey-Oyster 62
   Wild Rice 32
Cauliflower Italiana 36
Cheesecake, Old English 75
Cheese Bread 23
Chicken
   and Dumplings 56
   and Tomato Casserole 59
   Cacciatore Style 60
   Country Captain 57
   Crunchy Fried 59
   Easy Oriental Style 59
   Fricasee with Vegetables 56
   Livers and Mushrooms 58
   Mexicana 58
   Polynesian Style 57
   with Fruit 58
   with Mushrooms, Herb 60
Chop Suey, Chinatown 46
Clam Chowder, New England 18
Clam Sauce for Lingiune, White 30
Cobbler, Cherry-Pineapple 76
Cobbler, Spicy Peach 72
Cocktail Meatballs with Mushroom Curry Sauce 8
Consommé 20
   Double 20
   with Vegetables 20
Corn and Broccoli, Scalloped 40
Corned Beef Bake, Easy 49
Crab Casserole, Patio 67
Crab-Tomato Cream Soup 20
Cream of Broccoli Soup 18
Cream of Lentil Soup 16
Croutons, Cheese 15
Crust, Wheat Germ 78
Cupcakes, Carrot 74
Custard, Chocolate 77

Dressing
   Cooked Salad 12
   Creamy Cooked Salad 12
   Enchanting Fruit 13
   Gourmet French 12
   Gourmet Salad 13
   No-Oil Salad 12
   Roquefort French 12
Duckling with Orange Sauce, Roast 63

Egg-Lemon Soup, Greek 14

Farm-Style Leek Soup 17
Filling, Granola Cinnamon 27
Fish Fillets, Saucy 68
Fish Stew with Red Wine 70
Fish with Shrimp Stuffing, Baked 65
French Bread 23
French Onion Soup 15

Gazpacho Garden Soup 19
Giblets and Broth, Cooked 61
Glaze, Clear 6

Goose with Rice-and-Pickle Stuffing, Roast 62
Goulash Soup, Hungarian 15
Goulash Soup with Spaetzle, Hungarian 15
Granola Cinnamon Filling 27

Halibut Dinner, Planked 64
Herb Bouquet 70, 71

Ice Cream, Banana-Pineapple 73
Indian Pudding 76

Lamb
   Chops, Smothered 44
   Curry 45
   Crown Roast with Mint Stuffing 44
   Kabobs 45
   Leg of Lamb with Spicy Wine Sauce 45
Lasagne Bolognese 47
Layered Casserole 38
Lebanon Lentil Soup 16
Leek Soup, Farm-Style 17
Lentil
   Soup, Cream of 16
   Soup, Lebanon 16
   Soup, Tomato 17
Lemony Meat Sauce with Spaghetti 29
Lettuce Soup 19
Liver Pâté 6
Loaves, Mini 23
Lobster, Flemish Style, Mock 68
Lobster-Tomato Cream Soup 20

Macaroni Vegetable Medley au Vin 43
Minestrone, Baked 16
Mold
   Garden-Green Salad 11
   Peach Wine 13
   Spinach Cottage Cheese on Platter 10
Mulligatawny Soup 14
Mushroom(s)
   Baked 5
   Casserole, Broccoli- 39
   -Rice Casserole 31
   Wild Rice 32
   Wine-Pickled 8
Mussels Cooked in Wine Sauce 70

New England Clam Chowder 18
Noodles au Gratin 33
Noodles Romanoff 33
No-Oil Salad Dressing 12

Onion Appetizers 5
Onion Bread 23
Onion Rings, Lacy Cornmeal 37
Onion Rings, Lacy French-Fried 37
Onion Soup, French 15
Oysters Rockefeller 7
Oysters, Savory 67

Paprikash, Cabbage Rolls 36

Pâté, Liver 6
Peaches 'n' Corn Bread, Shortcake Style 72
Peach Wine Mold 13
Peasant Black Bread 28
Petits Pois in Rice Ring 33
Pilaf, Brunch 32
Polenta 29
Pork
  Bavarian Casserole 52
  Chops, Neapolitan 54
  Chops, Northwoods 54
  Chops with Beer Gravy, Breaded 52
  Ham and Noodle Casserole, Layered 53
  Ham in Claret, Apple-Covered 54
  Loin Roast 52
  Roast Scandinavian Style, Fruited 53
Potato(es)
  Deluxe Scalloped 41
  Parsley-Buttered New 37
  Puffs, Au Gratin 64
  Soup, Pioneer 19
  Soup, Puréed 19
  Soup with Sour Cream 19
Pudding, Indian 76
Pudim Moka with Chocolate Sauce, Brazilian 77

Red Cabbage, Sour 40
Red Cabbage, Sweet and Sour 43
Red Snapper Steaks, California Style 65
Rhubarb Swirls, Rosy 77
Rice
  au Gratin, Spanish 30
  Brunch Pilaf 32
  Casserole, Italian 31
  Casserole, Mushroom 31
  Casserole, Wild 32
  Loaf 31
  Mushroom Wild 32
  Pilaf Deluxe 30
  Ring, Petits Pois in 33
  Salad with Assorted Sausages 11
  Spinach and 42

Rock Cornish Hens with Fruited Stuffing 63
Rolls,
  Basic Dinner 24
  Bowknots 24
  Braids 25
  Butterflake 25
  Butterflies 25
  Cloverleaf 24
  Crescents 24
  Crusty Hard 25
  Fantans 25
  Figure Eights 24
  Kaiser 25
  Pan 24
  Parker House 24
  Snails 24
  Twists 24
Roquefort French Dressing 12
Rye Bread, Delicatessen 23

Salmon
  Broiled 66
  Rice Loaf, Two-Layer 66
  Squares, Baked 69
Sauce
  Bolognese, Meat 47
  Lemony Meat 29
  Mushroom Curry 8
  Orange 63
  Orange Ginger 7
  White Clam 30
Sausage
  and Applesauce Appetizers 5
  Supper, Hearty 55
  Supper, Super 55
Scallops Baked in Shells 71
Sherbert
  Cantaloupe 73
  Pineapple 73
  Watermelon 73
Shrimp
  and Rice Supreme 69
  Florentine 69
  with Orange Ginger Sauce, Puff 7
Sole with Tangerine Sauce 65
Sourdough
  Apple Kuchen 27

Avocado Sandwiches on 7
Granola Bread, Sweet and 27
Sam's Skillet Loaves 27
Starter 26
Spaetzle 15
Spaghetti Fromaggi 34
Spaghetti, Lemony Meat Sauce with 29
Spanish Rice au Gratin 30
Spinach
  and Rice 42
  Artichoke Casserole 42
  Bake 42
  Cottage Cheese on Platter, Molded 10
Spread, Baked Carrot 5
Stewed Tomato Aspic 11
Sweet Potatoes, Apple-Honey 41
Sweet Potatoes, Pecan 41

Tart in Wheat Germ Crust, Glazed Apple 78
Tomato Aspic, Stewed 11
Tomato-Lentil Soup 17
Trout Amandine with Pineapple 64
Trout, Broiled 66
Tuna Fiesta 67
Turkey-Oyster Casserole 62
Turkey with Herbed Stuffing, Roast 61
Turnips Custard 37
Turnips, Gingered 36

Veal
  and Vegetables, Curried 51
  Chops, German 51
  Cutlet in Wine with Olives 50
  Glacé 51
  Steak, Stuffed 50
Vegetable Salad, Mixed 9
Vegetable Salad with Yogurt Dressing 38
Vichyssoise 21

White Bread, Basic 22
White Clam Sauce for Linguine 30
Wile Rice Casserole 32
Wild Rice, Mushroom 32
Wine-Pickled Mushrooms 8